The
ANATOMY
of
CANALS

Decline & Renewal

The
ANATOMY
of
CANALS

Decline & Renewal

Anthony Burton & Derek Pratt

TEMPUS

First published 2003

PUBLISHED IN THE UNITED KINGDOM BY:
Tempus Publishing Ltd
The Mill, Brimscombe Port
Stroud, Gloucestershire GL5 2QG

PUBLISHED IN THE UNITED STATES OF AMERICA BY:
Arcadia Publishing
420 Wando Park Boulevard
Mount Pleasant, SC 29464

British Library Cataloguing in Publication Data.
A catalogue record for this book is available from the British Library.

ISBN 0 7524 2810 1

Typesetting and origination by Tempus Publishing.
Printed in Great Britain by Midway Colour Print, Wiltshire.

Contents

Restoration is still in its infancy on the Wilts & Berks Canal.

Introduction

In this final volume, the story is to be extended. Previously we had mainly been looking at the canals as originally built, how what we see today reflects choices made by engineers and architects working two centuries and more ago. Here we start with the last generation of canals, those built after the decline of the great burst of activity that had characterised the mania years. Yet, even as this late generation of canals was being built, work was already in hand to bring the first canals up to the standards expected in the nineteenth century. This need became imperative as a brash newcomer appeared puffing across the horizon, threatening to take trade away from the waterways and onto the new railways. There were to be some major improvement schemes put in hand during the nineteenth century, but even these were unable to do more than delay the inevitable. Canal traffic suffered with the arrival of the steam railway, but even more damage was inflicted in the twentieth century, when the internal combustion engine brought in a new, improved road-transport system. Commercial carrying is not yet quite dead, but it is a small fraction of what it was when canals were at their peak. If the canals had simply been allowed to die out as outmoded and worthless, that would have been the end – and this book would probably never have been written. But it was not the end. In the last half century in particular, there has been a massive resurgence in canal traffic; not carrying cargoes but holiday makers. The canals are busy with boats once again, and this has involved more than just a change in use; it has led to immense changes to the visual environment of the canals as well.

The use of canals for leisure has seen an interesting period of adjustment. Those who travel for pleasure often do so because they appreciate the historical context and take pleasure in the very special nature of waterways designed to meet the transport needs of the Industrial Revolution. This has created its own problems. How do you make a system designed for trade meet the needs of a leisure industry? How do you adapt canals mainly built in the eighteenth century, to the needs of the twenty-first century? This has become particularly important with the movement towards the restoration of old, derelict canals, where many original structures have been lost. There have been some imaginative answers, and one solution that is breathtakingly daring.

The world served by the canals has changed over this period of time. A classic example is Birmingham. At the start of the canal age it was little more than a village; today it is a major city. Inevitably the role of the canal itself has altered as well. Its old importance as a transport route gave way to a period when the canals that make up the Birmingham Canal Navigation system (BCN) were apparently mainly there to accept disused prams and supermarket trolleys, with the occasional dead dog for local colour. The growth of the leisure industry brought a new approach to canals, and quite suddenly it seemed Birmingham realised that what they had were not smelly ditches, but attractive assets. So, this book will be looking at a far longer time span than the previous volumes, and will take us up to the present day. Readers can decide for themselves whether the work of our generation matches up to that of the age of Brindley, Jessop and Telford.

1. The West Country

The area to the west of Bristol was among the last in Britain to see canals, and those that were built were not notably successful. One example would be the Glastonbury Canal, begun in 1827. It was built to link Glastonbury to the Bristol Channel, a distance of fourteen miles. It was, contemporaries recorded, intended for the export of agricultural produce from Somerset and the import of coal. Its opening was celebrated with the usual high jinks – feasting, speechifying and a procession of boats accompanied by a military band – but it never prospered. In less than thirty years, the canal had been bought up and its line adopted for the Somerset Central Railway, opened in 1854, which itself failed to survive the swing of Doctor Beeching's pruning axe. The truth of the matter was that no canal dependent on a mainly rural area was able to survive and prosper. If the Glastonbury Canal is a particularly startling example of brevity, it is not alone. Nevertheless, enough remains in the region to indicate that although the canals were largely unsuccessful as commercial enterprises, they gave rise to a number of fascinating engineering solutions to local problems.

The Grand Western Canal was the first in the region, and it has at least fared rather better than the Glastonbury Canal. Today, the canal is in water for a distance of nearly eleven miles, from Tiverton to a nondescript halt near Holcombe Rogus. The story of the Grand Western makes for sad reading, a classic case of misguided optimism. It was originally planned in 1796 as part of a far grander enterprise, the building of a broad canal that would link Exeter to Bristol, and then on to London. Fifty-ton barges would be able to carry out the whole journey without trans-shipment, but sadly for the Grand Western the connections were never made. It might have survived even then, but the story of construction is one of poor decisions by both engineers and proprietors. In the first plan, the canal was to reach Exeter and the sea via Topsham and to provide a northern terminus at Taunton. This would at least have provided a valuable route for much needed commodities, particularly coal from coastal colliers. In the event, the proprietors were seduced by the prospect of making a fortune by carrying stone from Tiverton. Originally, Tiverton was to have been served by a branch line, but now it was to be the starting point for construction. Work got under way in 1809, a mere thirteen years late. By 1812, the canal had reached Holcombe Rogus, delayed by the severity of the engineering works required to keep it on the level.

The engineer was John Rennie, and he used the well-tried technique of contour cutting where appropriate, and proceeding by bank and cutting at other sites. So, the route out of Tiverton is notably tortuous, with an immense U-bend round Halberton. The landscape was not the only problem facing the engineers. In 1811, the navvies rioted at Sampford Peverell, largely because they had found difficulty in getting paid. It lasted for more than twenty-four hours and at least two men died in the violence. It boded ill for the canal that there was not enough money to pay the contractors and the men. Beyond Sampford Peverell, the canal threaded its way through difficult, undulating countryside, with a final section cut out of the hillside. This part was opened for traffic in 1812, and the eleven miles had already cost more than the estimate for the whole forty-six mile canal. Here, for a time, all came to a halt. The good news was that the open section was lock free, and there was a steady trade in stone. Evidence for this can be seen in the limekilns beside the Tiverton basin, and in the many excellent bridges, constructed of sandstone, which can be seen along the way. Other evidence is not so immediately apparent. At Westleigh, one can see why it succeeded for a time – and why it later failed. A tramway swept down from the quarries to the north to arrive at a substantial wharf. With the arrival of the railway, a bridge was constructed of steel on rounded stone piers, taking the stone straight over the canal and down to a

The earliest section of the Grand Western Canal is notable for contour cutting, typified by the sweeping bend at Halberton.

John Rennie, chief engineer of the Grand Western, managed to keep the canal at one level, but this involved some heavy engineering works, such as here at Waytown tunnel.

siding and limekilns. But even without the loss of trade to the railways, this first part of the canal was never as profitable as the optimists had hoped. This is the section still in water, and which can be easily visited, running from the Tiverton basin to a dead end just beyond the short Waytown tunnel. The latter has no towpath, but remains of a chain used to pull boats through can still be seen. The most interesting features, however, are to be found on the now abandoned continuation to Taunton.

It was an Exeter engineer, James Green, who had already achieved something of a reputation for canal building in the region, who proposed the extension. It made a great deal of sense because a new canal had recently been constructed, the Bridgwater & Taunton, linking the latter to the sea via the River Parrett. By joining the new canal, the Grand Western too would have what it by now rather desperately needed, a useful connection with the rest of Britain. The first section of canal had been built all on one level, but that luxury was no longer available. Green, however, proposed building a lock–free canal anyway. He would overcome the hills and valleys by other means. He proposed an inclined plane and seven vertical lifts, built to his own design. The canal was opened to Taunton in 1838 and life appeared somewhat rosier, but only for a very short time. The Great Western Railway (GWR) empire was expanding. By 1844 Taunton had been linked to Exeter and four years later, even more ominously, a branch line was in place to Tiverton. Railway and canal were in direct competition; the GWR was growing and developing; the canal had never paid a dividend from the day it opened. There was only ever going to be one winner. The GWR leased the canal and eventually took it over. They promptly closed the line from Taunton to Holcombe Rogus, but preserved the earlier section for its continuing value in shifting stone. Even so, the canal Bradshaw Guide 1928 recorded that two stone boats, joined together by chains, were the only vessels at work. That was, in fact, the sum total of all traffic on the Grand Western, at that time.

Given the fact that the Taunton end has been closed since 1863, one might expect it to have vanished without trace, but in fact there is still a surprisingly large amount to be seen, particularly in the valley of the Tone. The top of the incline can be clearly seen at Wellisford (181/102217) as a footpath leading from a dead-end road up to the village, but please note that the incline itself is on private land. It was intended for use by tub boats, and these were counterbalanced by large buckets of water, rising and falling in a shaft. There were two sets of rails for double working. Excess water from the shafts drained away into the canal through adits which can still be seen at the foot of the slope. The system was not a success and was soon replaced by a more conventional steam engine for haulage, the engine house for which stands at the top of the incline (now converted into a cottage). There are remains of some of the lifts, including one just north of the goods yard in Taunton, but the most rewarding area for exploration is around Nynehead, where the old towpath provides another convenient footpath. An obvious starting point is on the minor road to Nynehead from Wellington, where there was a wharf and the wharf cottage has survived as a plain, but attractive vernacular building. Just a little to the east, the canal crosses the Tone on a simple aqueduct, which still has its trough of cast iron plates in position.

The horse-drawn narrow boat offers romantic trips on the Grand Western, but at the end of the canal's working life the only traffic was stone, carried in tub boats.

Firepool lock joins the Bridgwater & Taunton Canal to the River Tone, and was once also connected to the Grand Western. The former Great Western Railway building in the background is a reminder of what killed trade on the canal.

Further along the path to the west of the cottage are the best preserved of the lifts (181/145219). It now appears that the canal comes to an abrupt halt at a high wall, but recent excavations have revealed a great deal about the working of the lift. The caissons themselves descended into a pit below the level of the canal, and boats entered through a lock that could be used to equalise the levels. This was a counterbalance system, with wheels set above a central pier (now absent). Canal water was added to the upper caisson to allow it to fall, while raising the lower caisson. The foundations of cottages for the lift operators have also been revealed. Nearby is another aqueduct, this time altogether grander, making a bold architectural statement. Basically it is still an iron trough aqueduct, embellished with ashlar. The abutments are curved and decorated with pilasters, to finish off the grand effect. When something this grand appears on a canal it is a good bet that it was built to please a local big-wig. Sure enough, the aqueduct turns out to lie across the drive of Nynehead Court. The family insisted that the canal be out of sight, so the canal company not only had to build the aqueduct, but pay for the drive as well – the adjoining railway bridge and lodge are evidence that even Brunel lost this argument and had to foot the architectural bills. The canal line remains clear, set on a high embankment, but then disappears under an old land-fill site.

The Grand Western Canal is certainly a real curiosity. Having built the first part, which was the bit expected to show a profit, and notably failing to do so, the proprietors might have considered it prudent to stop at that. But then, when the railway age was already well under way, they started again. If it was folly to embark on an extension, it looks even more foolish to use a new and unproven technology. But then, even the great Brunel whose Great Western Railway finished off much of the Grand Western, was not above creating the odd catastrophe of his own. The Grand Western is not so very far away from the equally unsuccessful atmospheric railway that was intended to run between Exeter and Plymouth. The first train to use the system, which was rather like fastening a train to a giant vacuum cleaner, ran in 1848, and by the end of the year it had all been abandoned in favour of conventional locomotives. Perhaps, the canal didn't do so badly after all.

The Bridgwater & Taunton Canal had a somewhat complex beginning. It was always intended to provide Taunton with access to the sea, but it was originally tied to the abortive attempt to create the English and Bristol Channels' Ship Canal and was to start on the Avon near Bristol. The Act was passed in 1811, but by 1824

Bridgwater Dock provided a trans-shipment point between canal craft and larger vessels from the Bristol Channel. Today it is a marina surrounded by new housing, but the animal feed mill is still in use, and the tall chimney shows that it was originally steam powered.

the ambitious plans had been set aside in favour of a more modest proposal. Now the canal would start by the inland port of Bridgwater on the tidal River Parrett, an altogether more modest affair, just over fourteen miles long. There are five locks on the canal for vessels 54ft by 13ft. When the canal was first constructed, activity at Bridgwater was concentrated on the quays along the river below the town bridge. They are still there with their cast iron bollards. However, in 1841, a major improvement scheme was put in hand with the creation of a new dock complex. A tidal basin was created, joined to the river by a lock and a second lock led into an inner basin, where water levels remained constant. Vessels up to 180ft long could use the new docks and the canal was now rerouted to join the western end of the inner basin. As with so many small docks and harbours, now that trade has ended the docks have become a centre for development, with a marina and modern housing. The canal was later joined by the Great Western Railway, which crossed the navigable portion of the Parrett on an unusual telescopic bridge. In time, the GWR was to buy up the canal but now, in a reversal of fortunes, the railway has closed and the canal reopened. Bridgwater itself was an important industrial centre and the remains of a glass cone and brick works can still be seen near the canal. They provided just the sort of bulk cargo on which the canal thrived.

Charlton engine house was originally built for a steam engine to supply the Bridgwater & Taunton Canal with water from the River Tone.

There were few engineering problems in building this canal, which leaves the Parrett valley only to find an equally comfortable course along the valley of the Tone. The river provided water for the canal via a steam pump, the remains of the red brick engine house still being visible at Charlton. At Creech St Michael, the canal passes under the main road on a single-arched brick bridge, one of the few major structures along the way. Just to the west of it is the junction with the now disued Chard Canal. One survivor from that canal is the fine stone aqueduct across the Tone. The canal ended its modest fourteen-mile run at a junction with the Tone in Taunton, the top lock standing just above the river weir. It was later to be joined to the Grand Western.

Moving westward back into Devon brings an interesting variety of canals, some of which were short, privately financed and built to do just one specific job. The Cann Quarry Canal, for example, was just two miles long, built by the Earl of Morley in 1829 to join his quarry to a tramway at Marsh Mills on the outskirts of Plymouth. Lord Clifford's Hackney Canal of 1843 was even shorter, little more than half a mile. This carried clay, not stone, to the River Teign near Newton Abbot. The Stover Canal is the earliest, built between 1790 and 1795 by James Templer, who lived at Stover House, hence the name. It too joined the Teign at Newton Abbot, and once again stone was the major cargo. There is not a lot of the canal left, and what there is remains largely inaccessible, but there are plans being put forward for restoration. No canal these days, it seems, is beyond consideration. If it is difficult to see the canal, it is possible to see the quarries and the unique tramway system that fed stone down to it. Up on Haytor Down, to the north of the tor itself, are the very substantial remains of the Haytor Granite Tramway. Iron was an expensive commodity to bring all the way to Dartmoor, but stone was there for the asking. The engineers took the very sensible decision to build their rail system using granite 'rails', and there they remain, including junctions, snaking off across the open moor. Here triangular metal plates were installed which could be swivelled to allow trucks to turn off one line on to another. These canals may have become almost forgotten features in the landscape, but in their day they made a valuable contribution to the local economy.

A rather more ambitious project was put in hand by Lord Rolle in 1823, when he planned a six mile long canal from Bideford to Torrington, where he had lime kilns. This involved considerable engineering works, including an inclined plane at Weare Gifford, originally powered by a waterwheel. Quite the most impressive feature, however, is the Rolle or Beam aqueduct across the River Torridge. The engineer was James Green, as on page 12, and he produced a very fine structure indeed. It crosses the river on three tall arches, with relieving arches to either side. The rounded cutwaters are extended up to the parapet as columns, giving it a restrained classical appearance. Although the canal has gone, the aqueduct survives in such good condition because it still serves as a bridge carrying the driveway to Beam House.

One of the more unusual canals in the region, and indeed in Britain, is the Tavistock Canal. It is only four and a half miles long, but a third of that distance is in a tunnel. Construction lasted from 1803 right through to 1817, which may make this appear the ultimate in canal madness. But this is far from the case. The engineer

The final link between the Tavistock Canal and the Tamar was via an inclined plane and tramway. Part of the tramway, rising high above the docks, has been recreated at Morwellham Quay.

was John Taylor, one of the most distinguished mining engineers in the south west. The Wheal Friendship Mine had opened up near Tavistock in 1796, and the main purpose of the canal was to take ore down to the quays on the Tamar at Morwellham. Taylor, however, was convinced that there was more ore to be had under Morwellham Down, and so the canal tunnel was also used to explore the nature of the minerals deep underground. The result was the opening up of the profitable Crebor copper mines. The mile and a half long tunnel had to be cut through solid rock; not surprisingly therefore, it was built with modest dimensions, only able to take boats carrying a maximum of 8 tons. The thirteen years of hard toil were rewarded in that, unlike most of the south-western canals, it actually made a profit, if not a very large one. The figure does not, however, cover the profits made from the ore itself, discovered during the long years of excavation.

The obvious starting place for looking at the canal is Tavistock itself. The former basin is now a town centre car park, but the old warehouses and offices have survived. The buildings are mainly typical of the region, built out of slate stone, which tends to come in irregular blocks giving a very distinctive texture to the walls. This contrasts with the smoother, slit slates used on the roofs. The wharf office, by contrast, appears more sophisticated, with pointed Gothic windows. The towpath can be followed to a modest aqueduct across the Lumburn River before it disappears underground. It re-emerges high on the hillside above Morwellham. Here one can easily see the incline, with its slate sleeper blocks, leading to the river over 200ft below. Morwellham itself has now become a major open-air museum, relating the history of the port and the surrounding mines. The canal did have one short branch, out to quarries above Tavistock at Mill Hill. The branch was largely replaced by a tramway in 1844. Navigation on the Tamar was continued upstream by means of the Tamar Manure Canal, built in 1796. It began near Gunnislake, and there was a lock and basin at Weir Head. The name tells only a part of the story for the canal carried many other commodities apart from manure. It was just three miles long, but survived right through to the 1940s, showing a good profit for much of the time. There is not much of the canal left to see, but at least one of the Tamar manure barges has survived, and in spite of the unappetising name it is a very handsome vessel. *Shamrock* was built at Devonport in 1899 as a sailing barge, making voyages down the tidal river to Plymouth. She was later converted to a ketch when a new false keel was added, enabling her to go out to sea. She has a permanent berth at Cotehele Quay, where there is a small maritime museum. It is well worth a visit, if only to serve as a reminder of just how important these largely forgotten canals once were.

The name 'manure' did not necessarily mean the droppings of farmyard animals, but referred to any fertiliser. Sea sand was much in demand by the farmers of Cornwall and Devon, particularly where there was a very high shell content. This is not surprising, for it was very similar in that respect to limestone. One important source was Bude Haven, where in the nineteenth century a traveller recorded they were taking 4,000 horse loads from the beach in a day. That busy man James Green had the job of devising a canal that would take the sand to the interior. It was an immense undertaking, since the canal was to finish at a height of 450ft above sea level. Green, as we have seen, was not a man greatly enamoured of locks, and on this canal he had every excuse to go for the alternative option. He took the chance and created a unique canal system.

The canal begins at Bude, and in order to provide access to the sea, an embankment was constructed out into deep water and an entrance lock built inside it. The embankment leads out above the high water mark to a basin. The sea lock had turned Bude Haven into a small port, for now vessels up to 100ft long by 25ft beam could pass to sheltered waters, and safety has always been at a premium on this tempestuous coast. It was so successful, that both lock and basin were enlarged, first in 1836 and again in 1856. Large vessels could not, however, get very far. James had conceived his waterway as a hybrid. After a quarter of a mile, the canal narrowed down to take modest sized barges and then, after just over two miles, the climb began and barge movement ended. The entire canal, with its three branches, was thirty-five and a half miles long and included six inclined planes. The first appears at Helebridge. It is slightly disconcerting to walk the towpath from Bude along a perfectly conventional canal and to be suddenly presented with a small wharf and an apparent full stop at the foot of a steep hill. However, the route can still be followed

The canal above the lock at Bude. The walkers beside the lock are following the line of the light railway that was used to bring sand from the beach to the boats, to be sent on as fertiliser.

Although the Bude Canal above the lock is built to generous dimensions, the rest of the journey was carried out by tub boats because of the inclined planes that start after just two miles.

up the incline, and at the top are the remains of a wheel pit. The incline is 800ft long with a 120ft rise and, like most of the Bude inclines, was originally worked by a waterwheel, in this case 50ft in diameter. The vessels were tub boats, as used with earlier inclines, each able to carry a modest 5 tons. The next incline at Hobbacott Down is even bigger, 935ft with a 225ft rise. James, ever eager to experiment, tried a different system here. The tub boats ran on two railed tracks. They were provided with iron wheels and were attached to chains on the incline. As with his lifts on the Grand Western, James used buckets, 8ft in diameter dropping down a 225ft deep shaft to lift the boats. The waterwheels and hydraulic lifts demanded a steady supply of water, so a reservoir was constructed at the summit of the canal, which has now become known as the Tamar Lake. When the canal stopped work in the 1890s, the reservoir found a new role in water supply. All in all this is a most rewarding canal to explore – and provides excellent exercise.

Cornwall's other important canal, the Liskeard and Looe, was first suggested right back in the 1760s, but nothing happened until 1825. It had its northern terminus at Moorswater on the outskirts of Liskeard and followed an obvious course down the valley of the East Looe to the sea. There was nothing fancy about the engineering, simply a conventional fall through conventional locks and it enjoyed a great deal of success, carrying stone from the quarries of the Cheesewring on Bodmin Moor. This was later supplemented by copper ore from the mines of Caradon Hill, brought down to Moorswater on the Liskeard & Caradon Light Railway. Looe is now known as a picturesque holiday resort, but in the nineteenth century the port was greatly extended to cope with the increased traffic carried down the canal. A new warehouse had to be constructed on the quay around 1850 and is now one of the few reminders of the importance of the canal trade. Prosperity for the canal was not to last. The Light Railway that had helped bring in the trade was converted from horse haulage to steam power and was extended, reaching Looe in 1860. The canal struggled on into the early twentieth century, then succumbed. Not surprisingly, little remains to be seen after a century of disuse, though a lock chamber can easily be identified close to St Keyne Station. Nevertheless, there is an interesting story to be discovered here, of the intimate connection between Cornish industry and transport changes that all took place within a century. The line of the old tramway and railway can still be traced from the Cheesewring quarries on Bodmin Moor and even more dramatically as the lines sweep round the north side of Caradon Hill from Minions, passing through a landscape of spoil heaps and engine houses. Moorswater shows little traces of the canal basin, though there are still remains of lime kilns. However, something the area does have is a sharp reminder of the forces that overwhelmed the canal. When Brunel brought his Great Western tracks across the Tamar, the valleys were crossed by timber viaducts. The stone piers of the first generation viaduct stick up like tree stumps at Moorswater, while the more modern replacement is still an immense structure. The golden years of canals in Cornwall were short-lived, but were none the less important, as the evidence still indicates.

2. A Late Flourish

The opening of the Stockton & Darlington Railway in 1825 was not so much a warning call as a fanfare of trumpets, announcing that a new age was being born. Tramways were well established by then as valuable feeders, bringing goods to rivers and canals. Even the advent of the first successful steam railway at Middleton Colliery, Leeds, in 1812 posed no threat, as it was designed to bring coal to the Aire & Calder Navigation. The Stockton & Darlington was on an altogether grander scale, offering transport for a wide variety of goods and was even carrying passengers. The interest it aroused was comparable to the excitement caused by the opening of the Bridgewater Canal in the previous century. That ushered in the first great rush of canal construction; the Stockton & Darlington was to do the same for railways. The older generation of engineers, notably Thomas Telford, were alarmed by the signs. They still saw the canal system as viable, the most efficient way of moving bulk cargoes. They were quite happy to have railways that continued the old tramway job of feeding the canals, but did not favour any form of direct competition. What was now obvious was that the timidity shown in the early years reduced the chances of beating off the challenge. The narrow canals could not be fundamentally changed without huge investment, and the technique of contour cutting made for unnecessarily long journey times. The shortest route between the rapidly growing industrial centre of Birmingham and its network of narrow canals, and the equally rapidly expanding port of Liverpool was via Wolverhampton, the meandering Staffs & Worcester and the wayward Trent & Mersey. If canals were to compete, they had to come up with a better solution. It was against this background that the Birmingham & Liverpool Junction Canal was promoted. Work began under Telford with the passing of the Act in 1826.

Given the extent of the Midland narrow canal network, Telford saw no point in trying to build to any other dimensions, so this was to be a canal with narrow locks. Everything else about it, however, was to be completely modern. The route runs from a point on the Staffs & Worcester, near the bottom of the Wolverhampton locks at Autherley, to join the Chester Canal at Nantwich. From Chester itself, the final section of the route would use the new Ellesmere Canal and big improvements were to be put in hand beside the Mersey at Ellesmere Port. The new route was not only shorter but was carefully planned for efficient running by having far fewer locks, and having these grouped together in flights. It was to make for considerably shorter journey times, but it all came at a heavy price. The new canal was to have engineering works on an unprecedented scale.

As always when considering how and where a canal line was laid, an ideal starting point is the modern Ordnance Survey map. Two things become clear very quickly.

Stretton aqueduct is basically a standard cast-iron aqueduct, but Telford embellished it with ornate pillars and had his own name cast in the centre plate to mark an important road crossing.

The first is the proliferation of contour lines, indicating a hilly, hummocky landscape. If this had not deterred the first generation of canal engineers, it might nevertheless have induced them to opt for a rather wandering line to keep a level as easily as possible. This does not happen here. There are bends, but there are also long straights, cutting right across the contours. Between Autherley Junction, the southern end of the route, and Nantwich there are only twenty-nine locks in thirty-nine miles, so the hills have not been overcome by lock building. What we are looking at is the classic example of cut and fill. Deep cuttings were made through the rising ground, and the spoil carried away to build embankments across the valleys. It was work that was to give the builders immense problems. The second feature clear from the modern Ordnance Survey map is that there is very little here in the way of big towns, and certainly no towns of the type that might provide the bulk cargoes on which canals thrived. That meant that there was no need for Telford to go out of his way to reach those settlements and he could opt for the best engineering line. This was indeed just what its name suggested, a junction canal, where the termini were hugely more important than anything in between.

The start of the canal could scarcely be more modest. Those travelling this way by water through Wolverhampton, will have had a dramatic fall through a largely industrial landscape as the long flight of locks takes the canal down from the Birmingham plateau. By the time the bottom of the flight is reached, the scene seems wholly rural. There is a brief visit to the Staffs & Worcester in the gap between Aldersley and Autherley Junctions before the Birmingham & Liverpool turns away to the north. Here is a lock with a fall of just six inches, built purely to prevent water passing from the Staffs & Worcester to the new canal. There had been endless wrangling with the Staffs &

No canal made such extensive use of heavy engineering as the Birmingham & Liverpool, exemplified here by the deep cutting ending in Cowley tunnel.

Worcester who had resolutely opposed the newcomer, and now Telford had his revenge. The lock might have the smallest fall of any on the canal, but it has the grandest lock cottage. In Telford's own words, it was 'to awaken in the public a sense of the superiority in the new canal compared with the old'. The quiet, rural tone of the canal continues, apart from the modern intrusion of the M54, as the canal heads towards Brewood. This is a world of farmland and big estates, and big estates mean powerful interests. Chillington Hall is a fine Georgian house, built on the site of the medieval home of the Giffard family. The new house had its grounds landscaped by Capability Brown, who created an immense lake in a woodland setting. The approach to the house is down two long avenues, and the canal cuts right across the Lower Avenue. The gentry were not, on the whole, very keen on having canal boats pass through their lands, and even less enthusiastic about seeing them. So, the canal was planted with a screen of trees, and the stone bridge carrying the avenue was built of rusticated stone, decorated with pilasters and topped with a wide, ornate balustrade.

Cuttings are followed by embankments. The canal is dug into the top of the massive Shelmore embankment, pierced by a road tunnel.

Deep cuttings require tall bridges. This typical example crosses the Woodseaves cutting.

A hint of things to come appears at Brewood itself. The village is perched up on a hill, but the canal all but ignores the settlement. Instead, it carves in through the rising ground, so that all boaters see of the village are the towers of the churches, one Catholic, one Protestant, to either side. Telford showed scant interest in this attractive spot, being far more concerned in staying on his level and heading straight on towards his final goal. If in general he saw this as an essentially practical canal, where fripperies were only allowed when some grandee insisted, he was a man with a sense of history. Just beyond Brewood, Telford's straight-line canal was to cross the even straighter line of Roman Watling Street. Telford had a deep respect for the work of his Roman predecessors and this was a conjunction not to be overlooked. The aqueduct is a cast iron trough, consisting of five sections bolted together and supported on six iron arches. Telford's name was cast into the centre panel with the date 1832. And just to make sure no one overlooked the structure, the ends of the aqueduct are marked by handsome, round stone columns. It was perhaps a touch of vanity, but given his lifetime of achievements he had more than earned the recognition. On a more practical note, a small feeder enters the canal near the aqueduct, carrying water from Belvide Reservoir approximately half a mile away to the west. This supplies the almost eight mile long pound from the stop lock at the junction to the next lock at Wheaton Aston. Once again the canal does no more than brush the skirts of the village.

Beyond Wheaton Aston, the alternation of cuttings and banks begins, though modestly at first. The first major obstacle Telford encountered was steeply rising ground at Cowley. He planned a 600 yard long tunnel, but as the men began to break into the rock, they found it to be wretched, crumbling stuff, mostly marl and sandstone. In the event, most of the length was left open as a cutting, and the actual tunnel reduced to a modest 81 yards. This was ominous, for loose material of this type was to prove very difficult to stabilise and deep cuttings and high banks lay ahead. At Gnosall Heath, the Boat Inn shows in its plan that it was built to serve the canal, for it has an odd shape with a rounded end that enables it to fit neatly between the road bridge and canal. After that the canal takes a distinct curve to the south. It would be logical to think of this as a piece of typical contour cutting, such as one can expect to find on any canal. This is not the case. The map shows the canal cutting across contours, but curving to pass the edge of Shelmore Wood. This was the property of Lord Anson, and it was here that he raised pheasants for himself and his friends to pot at. They were not to be disturbed, so the canal engineers had to go round, not on the level as they would have wished but on a high embankment. It stretches for a mile and rises high above the woods and fields. It was to prove an immensely difficult and costly undertaking, and was not even to be completed in Telford's lifetime. The story of the embankment is one of endless trials, mainly unsuccessful, frustrations and disappointments. The engineers must have cursed those pheasants every day they arrived on site.

At first, there was little indication of what was to come. By 1831 there were 300–400 men at work and seventy horses bringing cart loads of spoil for the bank. The mound rose and sank again. The problem Telford decided was that the sheer weight

Tyrley top lock has a small cluster of houses and a warehouse. Telford prided himself on his architectural as well as his engineering ability, hence the pleasingly decorative stone surrounds to the windows.

of the wet marl was crushing the material underneath and forcing it out at the sides. The solution, he decided, was to use different, drier soil. Telford was now an old man and the work of the bank passed to a younger engineer, William Cubitt. He too found the soil slipping out sideways and proposed yet another type of soil to solve the problem. He was no more successful. Telford returned briefly to see the bank for the last time in 1833, but there was no obvious progress. Cubitt had to admit to the committee that the work 'has hitherto defied all our calculations as to the time of the completion'. There was nothing to be done, but to keep piling on more material until it finally consolidated. Telford died in September 1834; the canal was finally opened and boats crossed the Great Bank, as it was now known, six months later. The story of slippages and mud slides was repeated elsewhere, not just on the banks, but in the deep cuttings as well. Cubitt learned a lot about earthworks in a very short time, and was later to put it to good use. It is ironic that the canal that was built to

At the bottom of Tyrley locks, the canal emerges into a sandstone cutting, still showing signs of how the rock was blasted away with gunpowder.

challenge the railways should prove a training ground for the man who was to become one of the leading engineers of the new age. The banks are not so obviously impressive as the cuttings. Indeed, the scale of them is only really recognised from the surrounding area. A road runs along the south side of Shelmore Bank and cuts through it at the eastern end. Here the tall arch piercing the bank really does give some notion of the grandeur of the undertaking.

At the end of the bank is Norbury Junction. In 1835 a branch canal was completed through Newport to Shrewsbury. The canal is now largely derelict, but this remains an important point with canal workshops, pub and houses. This is a brief interlude before the next major engineering feature, the mile and a half long Grub Street cutting. Here the immensity of the undertaking is immediately obvious. The sides of the cutting rise alarmingly steeply to either side, and the cutting itself appears permanently dark and dripping. The sense of height is emphasised by the tall bridges, one of which has a double arch counteracting the inward thrust from the abutments. Trees and shrubs have grown up the bank sides, holding the material together, but in the early years slippage was a recurring problem. Grub Street was to prove the most troublesome of them all. There are other examples of banks and cuttings along the way, notably Shebdon bank and Woodseaves cutting, which presented similar problems but not, fortunately for the hard-pressed engineers, on the same scale as Shelmore and Grub Street.

Knighton Wharf seems to exist for no obvious purpose, but in its day this was a busy spot. Cadbury's established their works here. The surrounding countryside offered good grazing land for dairy herds and milk was collected from farms and dropped off at small wharves along the canal. The milk was processed into evaporated milk, mixed with cocoa and sugar and sent on to the main works at Bournville on the Worcester & Birmingham. There was a regular trade using Cadbury's own fleet of narrow boats, which continued from the time the works opened in 1911 for half a century. It was an important part of the trade on the canal, if only because it was dependable and regular.

After that, the approach to Market Drayton brings the first flight of five locks at Tyrley. Even here, the work was not straightforward. At the top of the locks is a small settlement of cottages and warehouse, built in 1837, just after the opening of the canal. The buildings are generally plain, but the use of a light stone for window surrounds does add interest to the facade. The locks appear much as any other locks, but as you descend the flight you discover that they have been cut out of the rock, a rich, red sandstone. This is an indication of Telford's thinking. By going deep, he would be able to stay at the lower level for over four miles, before he had to take the next descent. It meant more effort for the canal builders, but less work and faster passages for the canal boatmen. Market Drayton is the biggest town along the way, but the canal again skirts the edge and boasts only a modest wharf. Market towns were not necessarily very good canal customers, though the site proved sufficiently appealing for a large corn mill to be built alongside it. The mill was originally powered by steam, and the canal-side site had obvious advantages, especially in

The old Farmers' Warehouse at Market Drayton has an unusual shape, designed to fit it to both the road and a site hemmed in one side by an early bridge.

supplying coal. A second wharf, Victoria Wharf was added at the edge of the town. Of the warehouses by the canal, the former Farmers' Warehouse is built like a giant wedge of cheese, not inappropriate for a town just on the edge of Cheshire.

The rate of descent quickens after Market Drayton. First come the five Adderley locks, shortly followed by the longest flight on the canal, the fifteen Audlem locks after which there are just the two Hack Green locks to negotiate before reaching Nantwich Basin. Locks bring lock cottages, and Telford exercised his architectural skills, using one of his favourite devices, recessing windows into arched openings that run down to ground level. The most important building group is at Audlem itself, though the old warehouses have long since been converted into shops and pub. Nevertheless, something of their workaday life remains in details such as cast iron window frames.

The canal misses Nantwich itself by some considerable distance, crossing the road into town on another cast iron aqueduct, this time without extra embellishments. The line ends at a junction with the old Chester Canal, described in Volume 1: *The Early Years*. After Chester itself, the route follows the line of the Ellesmere Canal to Ellesmere Port and the Mersey. Up until then the port had been just a basin with locks down to the river. Now Telford was to transform it into a highly efficient dock complex, which allowed for trans-shipment between river boats and the narrow boats. The idea of building warehouses out over arches for ease of loading was not new, but it had never been undertaken on such a scale before. Everything was planned with care by Telford, right down to the trapdoors let into the soffits of the arches which allowed loads to be lifted straight out of the boats and into the warehouse. The port developed a new importance with the opening of the Manchester Ship Canal (see p.76) but then went into decline. It would have been one of the great monuments to the canal age, but for a disastrous fire in the 1970s which left only a fraction of the original buildings intact. What remains is still of considerable interest and is now home to the Boat Museum. One survivor shows something of the later improvement to the dock complex. In the 1840s William Armstrong devised a method of using hydraulic power, water at high pressure, to work machinery, and set up a manufacturing centre at Elswick in Newcastle. It proved ideal for working jibs and cranes in docks. It was the Armstrong Company that in 1876 supplied the two horizontal steam engines that were able to deliver fifty-seven gallons of water a minute at the very high pressure of 750psi. It was this water, pushing against pistons, that provided the power. The advantage of hydraulic power was that the water could be fed down pipes to anywhere in the whole dock complex to work machinery. There was also the equivalent of a storage battery, the accumulator, a heavy weight that could be lifted by water pressure to store power. The hydraulic system may not be in use these days, but the splendid engines survive, reminders that the Birmingham & Liverpool Junction Canal was once both important and determined to keep up with the latest technology.

There was to be one other important connection. The old Chester Canal had always been intended as a link to the Trent & Mersey, but the latter showed no enthusiasm for the idea. The aim was finally achieved in 1833, with the opening of

Audlem was once an important canal site, with its long flight of locks and wharf with extensive warehousing. Happily, the old buildings have found new uses, including conversion to a pub, The Shroppie Fly, recalling days of fast boating on the Shropshire Union.

the Middlewich branch, a modest canal but an important part of the network. In 1845, the Chester, Birmingham & Liverpool and Ellesmere Canal companies were united as the Shropshire Union Railway & Canal Co. By now the railway age was firmly established and there was serious talk of filling in canals and using them as track beds for railways. In the event, this never happened, largely because railway progress in Wales was lethargic, and the canals continued to do good business. The Shropshire Union prospered, and like the Grand Union ran its own fleet of boats, over 400 of them by the end of the nineteenth century. This is one reason why so many of the structures were well maintained and grand buildings such as the stable block by the double locks at Bunbury, on the Chester section, were built. In this at least, Telford's dream had been realised: he kept the railways at bay.

Telford carried out the initial survey for another canal, designed to shorten the route between the Midlands and the North, the Macclesfield. The Act was obtained in 1826, but not without a few flurries of anxiety on Telford's part. Some of the proprietors actually suggested that a railway might be a more sensible option. In the event, caution won the day, and Telford passed the actual work of construction over

The canal is crossed by this skew bridge on the final approach to Nantwich. Looking under the arch, one can see how the bricks have been laid in diagonal courses.

to William Crosley. Selecting a canal instead of one of the new railways might have seemed a conservative choice, but the route of the canal is every bit as bold as that of the Liverpool & Birmingham Junction. It was to run from the Trent & Mersey, north of the Harecastle tunnel, to Marple on the Peak Forest, which would give access to Manchester. To the east of the area through which the canal would have to pass were the high hills of the Staffordshire moors and Derbyshire Peak District. The line chosen hugs the bottom of the slopes, but this is no simple contour canal in the Brindley tradition, though it does have its twists and turns. Here too Telford called for considerable engineering works to keep his level. As a result, apart from one stop lock, there are just twelve locks, grouped together in a single flight near the middle of the twenty-six-mile route. There is one big difference, however, between this canal and the Liverpool & Birmingham. The latter passed through a mainly agricultural area; the Macclesfield served industries along the way. Macclesfield itself was a major centre for silk manufacture, while Derbyshire had a thriving cotton industry. All along the way were coal mines and stone quarries. The canal both served an existing industrial world and was to encourage construction along its route.

The route begins at the southern end with a canal rarity, a flyover. It is surprising at first to find a canal that is heading north leaving the Trent & Mersey at Hardings Wood by turning south. It runs parallel with the older canal for a short way, then turns to cross the Red Bull flight of locks on an aqueduct, then crosses the main road on a second. Both aqueducts are built of blue brick, with contrasting stone for copings, cornices and quoins. The canal then proceeds to head in almost a straight line on the journey north. Hall Green has a stop lock with a fall of just one foot, and it might seem a little odd to have a stop lock so far from the actual junction. The explanation is that this section was officially the Hall Green branch of the Trent & Mersey. Until quite recently nearby Kent Green boasted a survivor of the old type of ale house that could once be found all over the canal network. The Bird in Hand qualified as a pub, though you would never have guessed it, as walking in was like entering someone's front room. Only beer was sold, and that was brought up in jugs from the cellar. There was never any form of bar. Nowadays we tend to think that we can identify canal pubs, even when they have been changed over to housing, but it is easy to forget that the needs of the floating population were often met by modest establishments such as this.

Canal mileposts are generally either cast iron or very plain. This example from the Macclesfield, however, is a splendid example of the mason's art.

One thing that the Macclesfield offers in abundance is scenery. From the start the view is dominated by the hill of Mow Cop, with its splendid ruined castle on the summit, creating a most picturesque scene – except that this is not a ruined castle at all, but a folly deliberately designed to create the effect. The hills had another significance for the canal builders: they were a source of valuable stone. Mow Cop itself was particularly well known for its millstone grit, a form of sandstone that gets its name from its use for grindstones. Further north, The Cloud, another hill that dominates the line of the canal, was such a valuable source of good building stone that the canal builders constructed a railway from the quarries to the works. It was to provide the basic building material for the aqueduct and locks at Bosley. This was just what Telford thought railways should be, canal feeders, so it is no surprise at the start to find a flat bridge which still carries the name 'tramroad bridge'. The next bridge is of a type which will become all too familiar to those who travel the canal, a swing bridge. The advantage of the swing bridge to the canal company lay in economy. Instead of building an arch high enough to allow boats to pass underneath, they could construct a platform, level with the roadway, which could be moved when boats needed to pass. The bridges themselves are quite basic, with recesses on either bank, curved to allow for movement. The disadvantage of the swing bridge is the obvious delay to canal traffic, which tends to become worse with the passing of the years. Because the bridge is pivoted at one end, there is a tendency for the opposite end to drop, which is counteracted by stays. Even so, many bridges do

Hall Green lock marks the official junction between the Trent & Mersey and Macclesfield Canals. With a fall of just 1ft it acts purely as a stop lock.

A working boat near Macclesfield. The illustration gives an idea of the hilly nature of the landscape through which the canal had to be built.

droop quite noticeably, so that they settle down on the stonework instead of gliding smoothly across. The canal company had to strike a balance between saving construction costs and incurring later expenses.

After taking a slightly curved course at first, the canal settles down to a surprisingly straight line. The surroundings are still rural, dominated by a few grand houses. Ramsdell Hall has lawns that sweep down to the water's edge. This makes a contrast to the landowners along the Shropshire Union, who tried to keep a distance from the canal that passed their estates. Here, it seems, the owners welcomed the appeal of what the earliest canal promoters had promised. In the pamphlet published to further the cause of the Trent & Mersey Canal over half a century earlier, the authors enthused over the prospect of having 'a lawn terminated by water, with objects passing and repassing upon it'. It was, they declared, 'a finishing of all others the most desirable'. It is a viewpoint that has only recently found favour, so that estate agents who not long ago tried to hide the fact that there was a canal at the bottom of the garden, now laud the fact and add a few thousand to the asking price. The canal carries on, passing the most extravagant of all Britain's old timber framed buildings, Little Moreton Hall, a house that seems to have been put together from a jigsaw with a few of the pieces missing.

The locks on the Macclesfield were grouped together in one long flight at Bosley, overlooked by the shapely hill, The Cloud.

Nothing much disturbs the steady progress of the canal, until it reaches the outskirts of Congleton, where it swings round the edge of the town, before heading east along the upper slope of the Dane valley. Of Congleton itself, little is to be seen, but during the diversion round the town, the towpath changes side twice, involving the construction of two changeover bridges. These are among the glories of the canal. The Macclesfield, once clear of Kidsgrove, has entered stone country, and dressed stone blocks are soon putting in an appearance in the bridges. This in itself makes them visually appealing, but here the attraction of well-cut stone is joined to ingenious design. The bridges curl in on themselves, so that the towpath is carried in a short spiral down one side of the canal, over the bridge, then back underneath in a smooth curve. These bridges are popularly known as 'snake bridges', but a more appropriate name might be 'snail bridges', so tightly are they curled.

Now the canal engineers had their major works to consider. First, they had to cross the Dane, then climb the hill for the approach to Macclesfield. The aqueduct is a plain structure, but reassuringly solid as everything on this canal seems to be. This is an interesting place to compare engineering solutions to the same problem. A mere twenty years after the canal builders had appeared on the scene, the railway navvies were at work on the North Staffordshire line to Macclesfield. The engineering here is far more aggressive. Where the canal curves to follow the river valley, the railway cuts through the hill to the south, then marches across the Dane and the canal on a viaduct and embankment. The canal, having crossed the river at a much lower level

The former Hovis steam mill is an excellent example of how old buildings have been converted to modern use, still retaining important historical features such as the boat hole.

than the railway, now has to climb up through the locks to reach its summit level en route to Macclesfield. This is fed by two reservoirs, Bosley and Sutton. What is no longer apparent today is that the area to the south east of Congleton was heavily industrialised, with both quarries and coal mines, in the nineteenth century. The canal company considered a branch line down to Biddulph, but in the event made do with a tramway. What is now a tranquil, rural canal was once busy with trade.

The canal cuts through the outskirts of Macclesfield, quite literally, for the town itself is mostly lost from view behind the high stone walls of the cutting side. There are, however, intimations of what is to come, as mills appear alongside the cut. The nineteenth-century mills were generally somewhat plainer than their eighteenth-century predecessors. Where the early mills often look like overgrown country houses, displaying that sense of elegant proportion which is the hallmark of the period, the later versions can seem glumly uniform. It is not so much a question of embellishment as proportion; something which the Georgians seemed to get right almost by instinct. The mill theme is developed in dramatic fashion as the canal approaches Bollington. Here the canal crosses over the town on a high embankment. Bollington is one of those huddled northern towns, which seem to try and pack as neatly as possible into the available hollows to avoid the winds tearing across the surrounding moor land. The result is a medley of streets meeting at odd angles to utilise the often awkward spaces. All this is very visible from the canal bank, and the canal provided a new axis for development. The grandest of the mills, Adelphi Mill

An impressive mill conversion on the Macclesfield at Bollington.

and Clarence Mill, arrived soon after the completion of the canal and both are consciously designed to create a grand effect. At Adelphi, the decoration, such as the pinnacles above the water tower, seem to have been stuck on as an afterthought. But Clarence has been designed as a whole, making its visual impact through its elegantly high windows and details such as the little Romanesque arches at the top of the stack. Bollington, the canal and the mills all work together, unified by the use of local materials and an understanding of how to build in stone.

The canal continues through an industrial landscape, once dominated by mills and collieries. The mining activity caused many problems for the canal around Higher Poynton, though once it was a valuable source of trade. A branch led off to a mine in the west and the canal here is surprisingly deep. This was not an engineering choice, but the result of subsidence, calling for remedial work to prevent it disappearing altogether. There is one last flourish, another high embankment, before the canal wanders into the modern suburbs of Marple towards the end of the line and a junction with the Peak Forest. Appropriately for a canal where the workmanship in stone is as good as you will see on any canal in Britain, the route ends with the last of the snake bridges.

3. The End of an Age

Telford had been very consciously attempting to keep the railway age at bay by trying to remove the more obvious shortcomings of his beloved canal system but even without the railway threat, canal construction was slowing down. By the end of the nineteenth century the more obvious routes were all in place, and those parts of the country which still had no canal were either in that state because the terrain was wholly unsuitable or because there was no traffic to be carried – not that the latter factor always prevented over optimistic promotions. London, however, was one city of major importance where there was still work to be done. For centuries, shipping on the Thames had been forced to cope with tidal rise and fall, either using wharves at high tide, or anchoring in the river to be loaded and unloaded by lighters and barges. It was less than satisfactory, and early in the nineteenth century work began on a series of closed docks, entered through locks, so that water in the basins could always be kept at a level. Telford was responsible for one of the finest surviving examples, St Katharine's, close by Tower Bridge. It was not, however, the first of its kind. The Thames makes a great loop round the Isle of Dogs, and this seemed an obvious site for enclosed docks. In the event two schemes went forward together, the West India Docks and alongside them a ship canal, usually known as the City Canal. Both schemes were to be executed by Telford's old mentor William Jessop.

The City Canal was, in reality, little more than a long dock. It was built to an immense scale with locks at either end, 193ft long, 45ft wide with 24ft of water over the sills at high water. The space between was used more for loading than for passage. In later years, it was to be enlarged, incorporated into an extended dock system and was to lose its canal character. Now it sits, overwhelmed by the glass and steel of Canary Wharf. All these developments, however, were to have an effect on the world of narrow canals. The Grand Junction had arrived in London, had stopped at Paddington and only made a junction with the Thames high up the river at Brentford. But the new centre of trade was now shifting to the east. What was happening downstream could not be ignored.

In 1812 the Act was passed authorising the construction of the Regent's Canal, which was to link the Grand Junction at Paddington to the Thames at Limehouse. The scheme was not just for a canal to link with the Thames, it also called for the construction of a dock, but there were to be many arguments over how big the dock should be, how it was to be joined to the Thames and what size of vessels should be able to use it. Although the fundamentals of the canal as a whole have changed comparatively little over the years, this is certainly not the case with Limehouse Basin.

The Regent's Canal is very much an urban waterway, but at Old Ford lock it passes through Victoria Park, laid out in the 1840s. The decline in traffic resulted in one of the pair of locks being cascaded.

The canal was to be a modest eight and a half miles long, but life was never going to be easy for the builders. It is one thing to try and construct a canal through open countryside, quite another trying to cope with a major, and rapidly expanding city. That goes a long way towards explaining why this short canal was not completed until 1820. Problems appeared right at the beginning of the line. The preferred route would have gone right through the middle of Regent's Park, but there were other plans for that area. It was being developed by John Nash to epitomise everything that was finest in Regency planning and architecture, with houses to the south, in particular, which were models of urbane sophistication. Boats loaded with coal and brick did not feature in the scheme: the canal was banished to the outskirts. So there is a brief opportunity at Little Venice to enjoy early nineteenth-century architecture before the canal disappears underground at Maida Hill tunnel. This has no towpath, and being a wide tunnel, boats were legged through by boatmen using 'wings', boards stuck out on either side of the boat, so that they could reach the tunnel sides with their feet. The spoil excavated from the tunnel was piled up nearby, then levelled out, under the supervision of a groundsman, Mr Thomas Lord, and yes, that is indeed the Lord's cricket ground, home of the MCC.

Now the canal has only a short way to go before reaching the park, but it arrives in a cutting, leafy and pleasant and not disturbing the views of the ladies and gentlemen who were moving into the new terraces and villas built by Nash and Decimus Burton. In fact, the north side of the Park is a later development, as one

Limehouse Basin has seen many changes through the years. One of the latest additions is the quirkily handsome control cabin beside the lock giving access to the Thames.

could deduce from the name, Prince Albert Road. The architects still used the same stylistic language, but had coarsened it. Not that this affects the canal traveller who sees very little of it anyway. One notable feature is Macclesfield Road Bridge. It was here, in 1874, that a boat loaded with gunpowder blew up, killing the occupants and demolishing the bridge. The pieces of the bridge were collected together and reassembled. The fluted iron columns which supported the bridge by the towpath had become badly grooved by the passing of countless towropes, so they were reversed, and now the original grooves are on the towpath side. Those who don't know the story must wonder why there are grooves on both sides of the columns. Eight years after the canal opened, the boating fraternity acquired some exotic neighbours. The Zoological Gardens were first opened in 1828, but the most obvious structure seen from the canal is the modern aviary designed by Lord Snowdon, which unlike earlier bird cages actually allows the inhabitants some room in which to fly.

Once past the park, there is a sharp turn-off by the entrance to the Cumberland Basin, now home to a marina. Originally, this was a branch line down to the Cumberland Market at Euston, so that this is actually a former junction. Now the main line of the canal heads north to the first locks, a flight of three barge locks at Camden Town. In the nineteenth century, this was an exceptionally busy spot, with timber wharves and saw mills lining the canal and a busy industrial world of foundries and boiler makers. The warehouse was specially designed to take beer

The Royal Military Canal at Appledore, a section now in the care of the National Trust. It was still considered to have a military significance in the twentieth century, hence the concrete pillbox.

The connection between the Royal Military Canal and the River Rother was lost when this lock at Iden was taken out of use.

The line of the Wey & Arun is still obvious, if overgrown, as it makes its way through Sidney Wood near Dunsfold.

barrels, with a somewhat smaller space devoted to corn – and there was a large brewery. Now there are market stalls where once there were loads of timber, and shops and bars and more stalls in the warehouses; yet something of the working atmosphere has remained. Canal features have been retained, including the strange, castellated lock cottage, a winch and a cast iron turnover bridge. Together with the double locks, one has a real sense of the importance of the canal. In the nineteenth century, this was still New Camden, and certainly from the canal point of view it is New Camden all over again. One of the more striking features is a modern version of the London terrace, so familiar in the surrounding streets. This time, instead of London stock bricks, there is a row of shiny egg-like structures in metal and glass. In more recent times, London and many other cities have been blighted by a dreary series of pastiche buildings, hiding a modern structure behind a Noddy Land facade. These Camden houses have, at least, the courage of their modern convictions.

The canal surroundings are now unrelentingly urban, and the locks come steadily with the descent to the Thames. The railways are a powerful presence, and one can still see the interchange wharves, where cargoes were exchanged between the canals and the LNER at King's Cross and the LMS at St Pancras. Here also one can find one of the more unusual canalside structures. In the 1860s Carlo Gatti decided there would be a demand for ice cream in London, but had a problem. Ice forms in winter; the big demand for ice cream comes in summer, and the refrigerator had yet to be invented. His solution was to build an ice house. Great chunks of ice were shipped over from Norway in the winter, unloaded at Limehouse and brought by canal to the ice house. Here they were stored in deep wells at an even temperature, ready for use. Now the building houses the London Canal Museum, and the building itself retaining many of its original features, is perhaps the most interesting exhibit of them all.

Islington tunnel was opened in 1816, and like Maida Hill, lacks a towpath. However, this is a longer tunnel, on the busiest part of the canal, so as early as 1826, steam tugs were being used to pull the narrow boats through. There is one other unique feature of this tunnel. It was the very first to be illustrated during the period of construction. A contemporary sketch shows the men at work, and a number of construction details can be seen. Along the floor of the tunnel is a double railway track, the rails themselves having a U-shaped cross section, inside which wheels can run. The trucks are no more than plain four-wheeled trolleys, onto which wooden boxes can be fitted. Spoil is loaded into these boxes, which are then wheeled away to be hoisted up the shaft, and then returned empty. The men are stripped naked to the waist and working with flares, and the tunnel profile is a horseshoe shape, and in the picture the brick lining is largely in place. At the far end of the workings, wooden centring can be seen for the construction of the arch. Travelling through, one has little sense of the overall shape, as the section above water level appears more or less semi-circular, and little detail emerges from the gloom.

An unusual bridge at Rowner lock on the Wey & Arun. The stone abutments of the original bridge were topped by the brick arch in the restoration process.

Another interesting Wey & Arun bridge, Bat and Ball; here the curve of the arch is followed right up to the top of the parapet before being extended in straight courses in the abutments.

A traditional lock restoration at Baldwin's Knob.

Coates lock on the Pocklington has recently been restored. The alternating courses of light and dark bricks emphasise the curves at the approach to the lock, and the gate paddle gear is unusual.

Once through the tunnel, one finds the next two basins. There can be few canals where important bases and wharves appear at such short intervals, and City Basin was once centre of two of the biggest carrying operations in the history of Britain's canal system. In fact, the basin was really more of a branch, originally running for two and a half miles. The carrying company, Pickford's, now best known for house removals, began their business in the eighteenth century with horses and waggons, and even in the 1790s when they had gone into the canal business they owned twenty-eight waggons, 252 horses and only ten boats. The coming of the Regent's Canal changed all that, as they established two main bases, one here at City Road, the other in Manchester. They ran fly boats, working non-stop by changing horses and crews, and were able to average 2mph for the whole run – and that included working locks and legging through tunnels. City Road was organised so that waggons picked up cargoes from the north in the mornings, and brought in the cargo for loading and despatching in the opposite direction in the evening. They had their warehouse on the south side of the basin, together with a count house where literally hundreds of clerks kept track of all the movements of everything from small parcels to bales of cotton. Pickford's, however, were a company determined to keep in front, and as soon as the railway opened between London and Birmingham, they began to close down their canal trade. In 1820 they had eighty boats and 400 horses; by 1848 they had none. That was by no means the end of the busy life at City Road, for the work was carried on by Fellows, Morton and Clayton. This was, in many ways, the commercial heart of the Regent's Canal. The steady fall through locks continues, and one bridge has been given a modern treatment. The former Laburnum Basin supplied coal to the local gas works, but is now used for pleasure boating. The bridge by the entrance is typically plain, with blue engineering bricks for the main structure and stone for the coping and around the arch to avoid wear. It has been decorated with mosaics, with trees as an appropriate theme. It is not something one would want to see spread too far, but it certainly works very well as an occasional bright moment along the way.

The canal skirts the edge of Victoria Park, not perhaps as grand as Regent's Park, but a very pleasant green space in between Hackney and Bethnal Green. Here the Hertford Union Canal turns off for a mile and a half run through three locks to reach the Lee Navigation, one of the first waterways in Britain to have pound locks, a true meeting of canals old and new. The Hertford Union was built in 1830 by Sir George Duckett, and brought benefits to both waterways. The Regent's Canal is now nearing its end at Limehouse Basin, where there is one further junction, with the Limehouse Cut, joining the Lea just above the lock separating it from tidal Bow Creek.

Limehouse Basin has seen immense changes over the years; indeed it has seldom stayed in one condition for very long. Even before it had opened in 1820, the plans had been changed several times, from a single small dock, to two larger docks, a ship dock and a barge dock to the scheme which was finally adopted, that of a single basin, with a ship lock in the entrance channel from the river and conventional canal locks on the opposite side. At that time, the original Limehouse Cut entered the Thames a short way downstream. The two roads that crossed the entrance channel

The original Drungewick aqueduct had to be completely rebuilt, and it is seen here nearing completion – an unfussy, practical structure in concrete.

had to be carried on swing bridges. The design called for a dock with sloping sides, so wooden jetties had to be built out from the sides. Almost as soon as it opened it became clear that Limehouse was a success and expansion of the water space began – rather oddly, the first crane was only installed in 1822. Improvements now included construction of new quay walls, more extension of the space in the basin and the construction of a separate barge lock to speed up traffic into and out of the Thames. By 1839, the first railway connection was being made, not in opposition to the canal but to work in conjunction with it, and the London & Blackwall Railway became an important part of the working life of the rapidly growing dock. The story of expansion continued through the years, and working conditions were improved by the introduction of hydraulic power when an order for new cranes was agreed with William Armstrong. It was a story of continuous improvement, and unlike many canal ventures, the Regent's Canal continued to prosper with Limehouse handling nearly a million tons of cargo a year in the peak years of the 1930s. The final improvement came as late as 1968, when the old Limehouse locks were closed down, and the Limehouse cut was diverted into the basin. It was a short-lived enthusiasm, for in 1969 British Waterways Board announced the closure of the Limehouse dock to shipping. It struggled on for several years, a rather forlorn spot used by a few pleasure craft prepared to risk venturing out on to the tidal Thames. An even more exciting adventure could be had by trying to enter the dock from the river, since as soon as the boat turns to make the entrance, the current catches it and tries to carry it on downstream. Only the very lucky or the very skillful get into Limehouse without a bump or two. Now everything at Limehouse went into reverse; cut back was the order of the day, not improvement. A new, smaller entrance lock, built of concrete instead of brick was opened in 1989. The area of water began to shrink. By now most of the old dockland was being redeveloped for massive office and housing schemes. The huge Canary Wharf buildings came to dominate the skyline, and developers moved into Limehouse. Warehouses went to make room for blocks of flats, mostly nondescript and dull, and by the dock entrance a development known as Victory Place was built: whatever victory was being celebrated it was not one of architectural innovation. It is all too typical of its period. It was fashionable to mock the Victorian penchant for mock Gothic and to deride the 1920s taste for stockbroker Tudor, but what is one to make of the modern craze for overgrown Lego? Much of the old has been swept away, including the original hydraulic pumping house, in spite of the fact that it was the oldest example of a building of this kind anywhere in the world. The dock master's house on the pier head has a charm conspicuously lacking in its successors. It has now found a new use as a pub. The basin has inevitably become a marina. There has been one positive development, the Docklands Light Railway was built on the viaduct at the end of the basin, and provides a wonderful view of this and the rest of dockland. One can see what was, how little of the old remains, and what has been built. Change is inevitable, and Limehouse Dock has seen more than its share. It is not change as such that is objectionable so much as the low standard of design of so much of the new. It does not have to be like that. The world of transport can still show the way, and there are few finer buildings in this part of London than the new stations on the underground extension. Look at Canary Wharf Station, for example, and you can see that it is still possible to combine function with elegance on a modern transport route, just as the canal builders did two centuries ago.

The Regent's Canal proved to be one of the most successful canals of the canal age, and certainly shines out among those constructed just before the emphasis shifted to the railways. The title of the least successful would probably go to the Royal Military Canal. It was begun in 1804 to serve a dual function. Britain was seen as being under serious threat of invasion from France, and the canal was to provide a communication system for the defending army and also act as a physical barrier to the advancing Napoleonic forces. There was, of course, no invasion. Just one year after work started, the French fleet was demolished at Trafalgar and all thoughts of a seaborne invasion disappeared. An Act of Parliament of 1807 was passed in an effort to make some use of the waterway by turning it to commercial use as both a canal and by building a road alongside, with tolls paid on both. The canal runs from Cliff End to the east of Hastings to Hythe, a distance of thirty miles. The overall line follows a very obvious route, staying with the edge of the rising ground bordering the Romney Marshes. There are, however, curious little kinks at regular intervals along the way. These are not engineering aberrations nor the result of bad surveying. The engineer responsible for the construction was Colonel Browne, assistant to the

The former warehouse at Canal Head on the Pocklington Canal has been very sympathetically restored.

Quartermaster-General, and his first priority was military. Each bend allowed a defensive force to control the straight section, which was all within range of their guns, and the kink gave a clear line of fire down the straight. Given the nature of the land, there are, not surprisingly, few engineering features of any note. There was a lock, now disused, giving access to the River Rother near Iden, and a lock cottage. As part of the connection system, there was a lock at Rye, by the junction of the Rivers Brede and Tillingham, which works two ways as the Tillingham is tidal. Another interesting lock can be seen on the canalised section of the Rother near Houghton Green. Scots Float Lock was built in 1844 under the direction of William Cubitt, and is again two-way as it provides access to the tidal river. The canal has long since fallen into disuse. The section between Appledore and Warehome now belongs to the National Trust, who run it as a nature reserve with walks along the bank. Hythe Borough Council obtained a short section which they maintain as a pleasant waterway for rowing boats and other small craft.

Canals in the south east of England have not, on the whole, been a great success as commercial ventures. A number of rivers were made navigable and canal connections created, to provide food for London and to carry commodities, notably coal, into the country, but the main emphasis was on improving the land. The Act for the Wey & Arun Junction Canal, passed in 1813, specified a toll of 2*d* per ton, per mile for materials such as dung and limestone intended for use as manure, but double that for other commodities – and that included limestone not intended for manure. It would be interesting to know how many boatmen offered the information that their cargo of lime was meant for building, so could you please charge me double. The objective of the canal was simple enough, as indicated in its name: to unite the navigable sections of the two rivers. It was completed in 1816 and was extended to Portsmouth by the Portsmouth & Arundel Canal, begun in 1823. Neither fared particularly well; the line to Portsmouth barely lasted twenty years, closed in the 1840s and the Wey & Arun was officially abandoned in 1871. Part of the problem lay with the fact that when the Wey & Arun was first constructed, it was seen as a useful route that would avoid the dangerous south coast, where ships were harried by the hostile French. The end of the French threat may have been good for the country as a whole, but was bad news for the canal. It would be wrong, however, to think of these canals as failures. The Wey & Arun was to succeed in precisely the job it was built for, improving local agriculture, and was even to show dividends for a time – though in latter years much of the traffic was in carrying materials for railway construction. In 1865, the Horsham & Guildford railway was opened, which actually ran alongside the canal for some six miles. This was direct competition with a vengeance, and competition which the canal fraternity were quite unable to beat. The owners took the sensible course of closing down their operation while there were still assets to be sold and funds to distribute. The most remarkable fact about the Wey & Arun is that a canal whose life ended at such an early date should now be well on the way to restoration.

As a canal specifically designed to link rivers together, it obviously made sense to build it as a barge canal, with locks able to take vessels up to 13ft beam. There were to be twenty-three of these in the eighteen and a half-mile run from the Wey at Shalford, just south of Guildford to the Arun at Pallingham Quay, north of Pulborough. For a late canal, the adopted line was quite timid. The engineer, Josias Jessop, kept largely to the river valleys, which did not make for a very direct route, and there were further problems created by the fact that the Arun Navigation was less than satisfactory. Something of its nature can still be gauged at the junction at North Heath (197/038214) where the remains of the tidal lock can be seen close by Pallingham Quay Farm. The river is, in fact, tidal below this point and its course is both narrow and tortuous, so that the actual canalised section must have come as a great relief to anyone coming this way with a laden barge. Inevitably with the passage of more than a century since closure, many of the original structures have crumbled into ruins or been removed altogether. The Drungewick aqueduct, for example, was a modest structure, originally planned by Jessop to be carried on two low brick arches. It was demolished in 1987. In 2002, its replacement was completed, a concrete span, joining two newly created embankments. The restorers have mainly committed themselves to returning the canal to something of the character that it had when built. This is very appropriate for this very rural waterway, and there is an excellent example very close to the aqueduct. Barnsill Bridge would scarcely call for a second glance from anyone familiar with canal structures. Its fellows can be seen all over the system. But all is not quite what it seems. This is a brand new bridge, actually constructed in concrete. It was then given an outer cladding of brick, and a stone parapet was constructed on top. The result is both practical and visually pleasing.

Much of the track of the canal can still be followed, and a trip boat now runs on the section in water at Loxwood, to give a tantalising glimpse of just how pleasant this rural waterway once was and will be again. Of its later neighbour, the Portsmouth & Arundel, very little of interest has survived.

The Pocklington Canal has something in common with the Wey & Arun, in that it was mainly intended for agricultural produce. The table of tolls begins with a long list of commodities and runs through and names a dozen different crops before ending with 'other heavy seeds'. Apart from that most of the other tolls relate to commonplaces, such as manure, building materials and the inevitable coal. It was built to join the main road just outside Pocklington itself to a junction with the River Derwent, nine and a half miles away. There were seven locks along the way, capable of taking barges and the sailing keels which were widely used throughout the waterways of this region. One of these keels was the last vessel to trade on the canal, much to the annoyance of the railway company that had acquired the waterway in 1848 and had no wish at all to keep it open. They were, however, tied by their statutory obligations to maintain the waterway for as long as it remained in regular use, so they hit on a sound scheme to rid themselves of this last, troublesome keel.

The Pocklington Canal has unusually elaborate bridges. The curved abutments end in neat round-topped pillars, a device repeated by curved pilasters to either side of the arch.

In 1932 they bought the owner a lorry, and gave it to him on the condition that he never tried to bring his keel on to the Pocklington again. So it gently declined over the years. It was all very sad, particularly as the canal had a very auspicious beginning. The engineer George Leather actually completed it under budget, a real rarity in the canal world.

This may be a short canal, and at present only half of it is navigable, though the towpath can be followed. It is, however, full of interest. The original lock mechanism for the lower gates was worked by turning a large hand wheel, looking very like the steering wheel from some small yacht – and in the course of restoration, replicas have been set in place. Leather saved some money by building swing bridges, which were again slightly unusual in having a pivot point comparatively near the centre. This uses extra material, but on a wide canal makes for much easier movement as the extra length gives good leverage. He was quite lavish with the fixed bridges, which show very fine lines and are as substantial as they are graceful. Perhaps the best example is Church Bridge, near Thornton which has curved wing walls, ending in circular pillars. As one would expect in this part of the world, the main structure is of brick with stone reinforcement at the arch and for coping. The theme of round columns is repeated at either side of the arch. Few structures of significance survive, but the former brick warehouse at Canal Head has now been converted into a private house. The lock cottage is also privately owned, but the lock keeper's pigsty is now home to the Pocklington Canal Amenity Society, who use it as an information point.

Another short-lived canal begun in the early nineteenth century was designed to serve Carlisle by creating a new port further to the west, to save vessels from the treacherous waters of the Solway Firth. The Carlisle Canal received its Act in 1819, and presented a number of interesting difficulties. One unexpected problem was the failure of the engineer, William Chapman, who had prepared the plans, to agree with the Committee, and he was sacked before completion. The main problem lay at the western end at a place called Fisher's Cross, later renamed Port Carlisle. There was a sea lock which provided access to the main canal basin, but the estuary is notorious for its very high tides. The engineers studied the records and found that in January 1796 one tide had risen 15ft 6ins above the average high water levels on the neaps. So, a second basin was created behind the first with a second lock. This could be used if the first flooded. After that, the canal carried on in an orderly manner, but with scant regard for archaeology, twice cutting through Hadrian's Wall or, as it was known at the time, the Picts Wall. A familiar story of failure to fight off railway competition followed soon after completion, and in 1852, the company decided on a 'if you can't beat them, join them' policy. The canal was filled in and a railway laid over it.

The remains of the sea lock at Port Carlisle can still be seen, together with part of a jetty which ran out to deep water, used by passengers for the steamer service on the Solway Firth. The lock itself was an imposing structure, built out of massive stone blocks. A section of canal can then be traced before the railway takes over, and the platform of the railway station appears. It too closed, when a new port was opened further west at Silloth. The railway is easily discerned, running to the south of the embankment that divides the settled land from Burgh Marsh. One does not expect to find much evidence of the canal, but some of the railway overbridges appear to have utilised the old canal bridges, simply raising them higher to allow for the new traffic. These are by no means the only canals to be built in the early nineteenth century, but some have such scant remains that it is no longer possible to say anything very meaningful about either their engineering or their architecture. There was, however, one area of Britain which saw immense improvements in the nineteenth century, and which is one of the few regions where commercial carrying continues right up to the present day.

4. Canals in the Victorian Age

The Aire & Calder Navigation has a history that stretches back beyond the canal age, right back to the river improvements of the seventeenth century. The first Act was passed in 1699. Up to that date vessels had been able to come from the ports of the Humber, up the Yorkshire Ouse and along the Aire as far as Knottingley. The Act extended navigation to Leeds and also allowed for improvement of the tributary river, the Calder as far as Wakefield. Altogether fifteen locks were built, eight of which were cut where weirs already existed to serve local mills, the rest requiring new weirs. They were of generous dimensions, 15ft wide and 60ft long, and from the start the navigation proved very successful, particularly in supplying coal from the South Yorkshire coalfield. It is no historical accident that the world's first commercial steam railway was built in 1812 to join the Middleton Colliery at the edge of Leeds to the Navigation. The Aire & Calder was, indeed, so successful a system that there was a constant demand for improvements.

In the meantime, work was going on further south, aimed at linking the growing industrial towns of Sheffield and Rotherham with the Humber, via the Trent and the Don. The first proposal for improvements was put forward in 1697, but was turned down, so it was not until 1726 that an Act was passed allowing work to begin. Before this, rather surprisingly for anyone who knows the region today, the principal port for South Yorkshire was Bawtry on the River Idle. Now, however, the Don was to be made navigable as far as the Dutch River. This, as the name suggests, had been originally constructed for drainage rather than navigation – and it proved to be considerably more suitable for the former than the latter. It was constructed by Vermuyden, who was responsible for a huge amount of drainage work in eastern England, and completed in 1625. The Don was followed upstream as far as Newbridge, where an artificial cutting was made to the Ouse at Goole. It was designed to run straight and true to carry away floodwater as rapidly as possible, which it certainly succeeds in doing, so fast indeed as to make navigation a perilous occupation in wet weather. The Dutch River succeeded in its primary purpose, and Vermuyden's name is still remembered in a pub name at the head of the cut in Goole. It was clear, however, that some alternative and more secure navigable route was needed to link the interior to the tidal rivers. The answer was to build a new canal, the Stainforth & Keadby, which left the River Don at Stainforth for a new junction with the tidal Trent at Keadby. That was begun in 1793, and in 1813 the system was further extended with the Sheffield Canal, which finally brought waterways to the heart of the city. These waterways eventually came together to form the Sheffield & South Yorkshire Navigation. All these waterways were designed with a particular vessel in mind, the Humber keel. This was and is just about the closest survivor to the medieval boat. It has a single mast, carrying a square sail and topsail, with a somewhat inelegant hull, similar in shape to a date box. This shape ensured that the keels fitted snugly into locks and maximised the cargo space. The last of the sailing keels, *Comrade*, has been kept afloat and is run by a preservation trust. She was a Sheffield boat, with dimensions designed to fit the smallest locks on the system, those on the Sheffield Canal itself, 61ft 6in by 15ft 3in. She is a delight to sail, and in spite of the blunt bows and what might seem an old-fashioned rig, handles extremely well on the broad waters of the Humber. Inland, the sails were used if the wind was favourable, but otherwise the keels were towed by the so-called horse marines. There was to be one further link, which would unite these two important systems. In 1896, work began on the New Junction Canal, linking the Aire & Calder to the Sheffield & South Yorkshire. It runs for just over five miles, and is ruler straight. It has just one lock in the middle, and very plain aqueducts at either end, crossing first the Don then the Went. There are no settlements along the way of any size, and the minor roads that cross the canal are all carried on swing bridges. The junction at Stainforth is enlivened by a row of canalside cottages, and the canal's one and only pub. Visually, it is probably the least interesting canal in Britain, but it proved to have considerable commercial value.

We have to look at the Aire & Calder first, not out of respect for its seniority, but because what happened here was to have a huge effect on the Sheffield & South Yorkshire. The Aire & Calder was a success, partly because it served an important and rapidly growing industrial area centred on Leeds, but even more because it had access

A pair of Tom Pudding pans, with the false bows in front, at Goole. Working barges can be seen in the background.

The last surviving coal hoist at Goole. The Tom Pudding pans were lifted to the top of the tower, then upended, so that coal went down the chute into the waiting ship; the chute is shown here lifted, but would be lowered when needed.

to a rich coalfield. It was even more fortunate in having a succession of managers and engineers who appreciated that continuing success meant continuing improvements. The immediate response to the railway age was to institute a huge modernisation programme. By the 1830s, the original main line had already been improved by the construction of a whole new artificial canal from Ferrybridge to the Ouse at what was to become a new port, Goole. Look at a map, and the advantages of what was also known as the Knottingley & Goole Canal are obvious. The Aire wriggles and squirms its way across the land, turning back on itself in immense loops, eventually joining the Ouse north of Airmyn. The locks along the way allowed for a controlled drop in level, but there were no long navigable cuts. The final part of the new canal closely follows the line of the Dutch River, the two running side by side for some five miles. It was not only the civil engineering of the system that was improved. In 1831, steam tugs were introduced, capable of hauling trains of barges. The efficiency of traffic movement was increased, but was limited by the size of locks, which were designed for barges, not barges plus tug. In 1860, Pollington lock was rebuilt to more generous dimensions and the rest soon followed. There were to be more changes over the years, and today the locks between Leeds and Goole are 200ft by 20ft. What marks out the Aire & Calder from other systems was the recognition that for a canal to compete in the railway age, everything had to be modernised, not just the waterway itself, but also the boats that used it and cargo handling. One of the great innovators was the company's engineer, William H. Bartholomew.

Bartholomew invented a system of compartment boats, which fastened together in a flexible train. In his first experiment in 1863, he used a specially built steam tug, a bit of a lash up with a simple two-cylinder engine and a boiler taken out of a locomotive. The compartment boats themselves were little more than open iron boxes, and they came to be known as 'Tom Puddings'. One theory has it that the name came from their resemblance to pudding pans, and individual boats are known as pans, another that the train of black vessels looked not unlike a string of black puddings. In Bartholomew's first version, the tug pushed the train, using an elaborate system of wires passing to the front pan, so that the whole assembly could be bent to go round corners. This proved unwieldy, and the simpler towing system was soon adopted. A new problem appeared, however, in that there was a tendency for water to build up in the confined space between the propeller and the first pan. This was solved by adding a false bow or jebus between the tug and the first boat, and that was the system that remained in use until the last run in 1979. What set Bartholomew's scheme apart from other improvements was the way in which he thought of the Tom Puddings as part of an integrated system, for moving coal from the Yorkshire coalfield to the new port at Goole. Loading the coal was simple, and could be done in the time honoured way by means of chutes at staithes. But at Goole, the coal had to be removed from the Tom Puddings and loaded into coastal colliers. He designed a system of hydraulic hoists. Goole was to have four fixed hoists and one floating hoist. Individual pans were detached, and floated under the hoist. There the whole pan with its load of coal, a weight of up to 52 tons, was lifted to the top of the hoist then upended to deliver the coal down a chute into the hold of the ship. Today, only one of these great hoists survives, preserved at Goole along with one or two Tom Puddings. Yet at the beginning of the century, there were a thousand pans in use, shifting millions of tons of coal a year. It was perhaps inevitable that a system devised in the 1860s could not last for ever, and I was lucky enough to see the Tom Puddings at work at the very end of their working lives. I met two trains of Tom Puddings on the New Junction, one working through Sykehouse lock. It was going down the lock, but even after modernisation, the train was too long to go through in one piece. There were fifteen pans, each holding 30–35 tons. The train was split and the tug hauled the first half into the lock and out again at the bottom. The lock was refilled and the top gates opened. The lower paddles were drawn, sucking the pans into the lock. It was slow and laborious, and goes some way to explain why the system stopped running very shortly afterwards. The surviving hoist at Goole looks like the sort of thing that children used to make out of Meccano, a spindly framework of riveted girders, and a system of chains and pulleys for the lifting and tipping mechanism, all topped by a utilitarian control box. It is impressive, but not beautiful. Nevertheless, it is a very important historical relic and every effort should be made to ensure its preservation. At the time of writing, it is in less than perfect condition. The ideal would be not just to preserve it, but to restore it to working order.

Goole itself is as much a canal new town as Stourport or Ellesmere Port, and like the earlier canal towns, this was based on a trans-shipment port, but on a much larger scale. George Leather was the engineer and surveyor. He designed a barge dock and a ship dock, to which a steam-boat dock and a railway dock were added later, all constructed on reclaimed marshland. The ship docks are still in use and barges still pass through, with cargoes such as sand from the estuary sent inland for construction work. The new towns of the early canal age had their share of Georgian elegance, but little of that is evident at Goole. This was a company town and everything was done that would add to its prestige, and not a great deal was done for the rest of the community. The houses that could be seen from the river and docks had a certain, rather glum, grandeur and were for the professional classes. In the town itself, out of sight and therefore not needed to show a brave face to the world, there was a regular grid of terraces. These are very much like the terraces of the Victorian mill town, basic and small. The worst of them have been removed in a slum clearance in the 1960s, but even those that remain have a huddled appearance. The company's own buildings such as the offices and hotel are quite grand in their way, but austere. Architecture was not rated very highly in the company's list of priorities, although they claimed it was to be 'in point of elegance and uniformity' the handsomest town in the north of England. The uniformity was achieved, but not the elegance. Being a company town, buildings that elsewhere formed a focal point, such as the town hall, were not needed. They even refused to build a church, and only succumbed after some twenty years of pleading by the residents. Today, although the docks are busy, the town has a sadly depressed air.

The story of innovation did not end with the passing of the nineteenth century. Lock improvement came with electrification: gates opening and closing at the press

Above and right:
Keadby lock is one of the last on the Sheffield & South Yorkshire to retain hand-operated paddle gear; the modern equivalent at Sprotbrough is operated with electric, push-button controls.

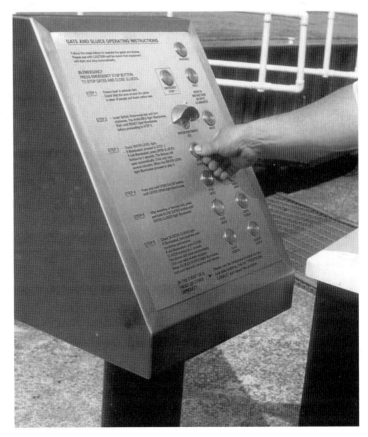

Aldwarke lock is one of the improved Sheffield & South Yorkshire locks, electrified with traffic lights to control movements. Once again, the control box shows the age-old qualities of neat design and appropriate materials.

of a button and movement controlled through lights. The control boxes are neat and practical, if not inspiring. And Bartholomew's idea for mechanising coal deliveries was taken a step further at Ferrybridge power station in 1966. Instead of Tom Puddings, 150-ton barges were moved in groups of three by push tugs, and the individual barges were plucked from the water by a hoist and upturned into the bunkers. The scheme was to be short lived, scarcely having a chance to prove its worth before coal was phased out. The last barge deliveries to any of the power stations on the Aire & Calder were made in 2002.

The other site of major importance is the western end of navigation at Leeds. The first artificial cutting makes a head-on link with the Leeds & Liverpool Canal, while the river roars away in very dramatic fashion under the arches of the railway station. Again, this was a busy spot until quite recently, and even the steam cranes on the Co-op wharf were in use right up to the 1970s. But, in general, there was an air of dereliction about the old warehouse and wharf area until quite recently. Now there has been a complete transformation. A number of elements have come together to change the outlook for the urban canal. Loft living, first popularised in New York, soon became very fashionable. Old warehouses were no longer seen as eyesores, but as buildings of character, ready for development as apartments or offices.

Previous page: 1. *Problems at Albert Street cutting, on the Grand Western, called for strengthening of the retaining wall.*

Above: 2. *Eckington Bridge on the Avon, its worn sandstone much patched over the centuries.*

Left: 3. *The Tavistock Canal tunnel emerging high above the Tamar at Morwellham.*

Right: 4. *The unusual counterbalanced ground paddles on the Bridgwater & Taunton Canal.*

Below: 5. *The entrance lock to the Bude Canal at low tide.*

Opposite: 6.
*The ornate bridge
crossing the driveway to
Chillington Hall on
the Birmingham &
Liverpool Junction.*

Above: 7. *A parking
problem solved – Lyme
View marina on the
Macclesfield Canal.*

Right: 8. *Red Bull
aqueduct carries the
Macclesfield Canal over
the ore-stained waters
of the Trent & Mersey.*

Above: 9. *The Regent's Canal reflects the opulence of housing at Regent's Park.*

Below: 10. *A neat new control box at Barnby Dun on the Don Navigation with a background of power station cooling towers.*

11. *Crown Point Bridge, Leeds, recently painted to bring out the details of the ornamental iron work.*

12. *Development of the area around Camden locks has brought crowds to the canal.*

Above: 13. *Anderton Boat Lift, recently restored to working order.*

Left: 14. *The M5 viaduct dwarfs the little Stewart aqueduct on the Birmingham Canal.*

Below: 15. *Leamington lift bridge on the Union Canal.*

Above: 17. *The Falkirk Wheel replaced a flight of derelict locks. The picture shows the upper caisson aligned with the aqueduct.*

Previous page, right: 16. *A magnificent jib crane, a reminder of working days at Weston Point.*

Above: 18. *Looking back down the canal from Sheffield Basin.*

Below: 19. *Cast-iron mileposts such as this were, in their day, the latest thing in modern technology.*

Right: 20. *A rare example of a modern lock cottage at Evesham.*

Opposite: 21. *The Glaxo
building at Brentford benefits
from its canalside setting.*

Right: 22. *The new and the old
in Birmingham.*

Below: 23. *The modern
footbridge and the Victorian
railway viaduct at Castlefield
Basin, Manchester.*

Above: 24. *At Banbury developers have opted for a pastiche of traditional canalside buildings.*

Left: 25. *Ground paddles at the double locks on the Trent & Mersey.*

Opposite Page

Above, left: 26. *The refurbished lock at Camp Hill Birmingham has been enhanced by picking out the heel grips in different brick from the surrounds.*

Above, right: 27. *Restoration is still in its infancy on the Wilts & Berks Canal. At Dauntsey the canal is in water while the lock is still being rebuilt.* (See page 6)

Below: 28. *The eerie charm of The Fens, Angel Corner, Whittlesey.*

29. *The Beam aqueduct carrying the Rolle Canal over the River Torridge is a remarkably fine structure for what is really a very minor canal.*

The entire area from the first locks down has been extensively redeveloped, the whole project having been started at Victoria Quay, the former terminal basin of the Aire & Calder. The basin itself has had its water level lowered, turning it into an ornamental pond, complete with fountains. One can still see the quality of the older buildings, such as the flyboat warehouse with its arched opening over the water. There is even an opportunity to learn something about the internal construction of the buildings, as roof trusses were removed and reused, keeping their form, as a footbridge. The developers converted some of the warehouses into apartments, but also provided new buildings, intended to reflect the character of the old. Other developments soon followed. At Merchant's Quay, the flax mills dating back to 1824 have been converted. These are just the sort of buildings which had been neglected in the past, but their fine qualities of well-balanced facades and mellow brickwork are now much appreciated. Even 1930s buildings have not been ignored. A group near Tetley Wharf has been transformed to look both traditional and modern by reproducing the old covered hoists as glazed extensions projecting from the main building and rising over a riverside terrace. Not all the new building has appeared as a pastiche. The Royal Armouries Museum architects have opted for an original approach, producing an octagonal glazed tower, looking not unlike a transparent lighthouse. Perhaps the best way to get a sense of what the Aire & Calder meant to Leeds is to take a walk down Dock Street. Here the brick warehouses crowd in on

A contrast in styles: the multi-arched Dutton viaduct soars over the Weaver, dwarfing the delicate footbridge that crosses a tributary.

Developments along the Aire & Calder vary from conversion of old mills and warehouses (opposite) to wholly modern buildings such as The Royal Armouries Museum (above).

Barton swing aqueduct replaced the original Brindley Bridgewater Canal aqueduct when the Manchester Ship Canal was built. Here it is shown opening to allow a ship to pass: an increasingly rare occurrence.

either side, their high walls closing out the light. To one side are the warehouses of Leeds wool and cloth merchants, the Aire & Calder's own buildings on the other. For those who knew the area before work started, the transformation is remarkable and the effect has been to change the city centre. People now live and work here and visitors can stay in hotels converted from the old working buildings. There is a real sense of liveliness to replace the rather forlorn air that hung over the area for too long. But progress demands its price. A new generation of tall buildings, designed, if that is the word, in the new corporate style of dull anonymity is rising up around the area, threatening to swamp the old and characterful. On balance, however, it has to be said that what has happened here has been a success. A similar care was shown when the ornate iron bridge over the waterway had to be widened to cope with modern traffic. Crown Point Bridge was built in 1840, with the roadway carried on iron arches, with an elaborate and very attractive fretted façade. Structurally everything has changed, with the enlargement of the arch, but outwardly it still seems the same fine example of Victorian bridge building.

There is more canalised waterway than natural river as the Aire & Calder makes its way over the generally flat landscape, with just thirteen locks in the thirty-four miles between Leeds and Goole, though there are another five in the branch linking the main line at Castleford to Wakefield and the Calder & Hebble. Bridges are few and one of the more attractive that carried the old Great North Road now sits under

Latchford locks. The Manchester Ship Canal had locks designed to pass vessels of different size, and even the largest locks had intermediate gates to subdivide them.

the shadow of its concrete replacement, built for the A1(M). The landscape through which the canal passes is still dominated by the remains of mining, flashes and spoil heaps and the occasional staithes for loading coal. It is, however, no more than a memory. Those looking for engineering excitement and architectural splendours will find little of either on the Aire & Calder. What one will find is ample evidence to show why the canal was a success for so long and why it still carries at least some traffic today. The other feature met along the way is the M62, which now takes much of the traffic that would once have gone by water. It is probably already too late to expect planners to consider that modern barges on a canal can move bulk goods with efficiency, and without clogging up already overcrowded roads.

Turning now to the Sheffield and South Yorkshire system, Keadby at the Trent end produces oddities from the word go. The river at this point is tidal and sometimes the water in the river can rise above the level of the canal. Ordinary lock gates, on their own, would be swamped and the canal would be unusable, so an extra pair of sea gates was added to cope with the highest tides. The entrance from the river seems alarmingly narrow after the wide waters of the Trent, but is made slightly easier by the rounded walls that provide the entrance to the lock itself. To describe the modern, red brick lock buildings as plain would be to flatter them. As this was a waterway that would be used by high-masted keels, all bridges had to be made moveable, and when the railway came along there was no exception made. The land here is all very flat, and the railway engineers had little space to build up an embankment between the river crossing and the canal, and little wish to do so. They had first to cross the Trent on their way from Scunthorpe, then the drainage channels of the Three Rivers, both of which could be met square on. Arriving at the canal, however, they were on the skew, so they took the unusual decision of constructing a bridge low over the water, but which could be slid out of the way to allow boats to pass. Once across, the railway swings round to follow the line of the canal very closely all the way to Thorne, nine miles away. There is, it has to be admitted, not a great deal to excite interest as the canal makes its steady way, with just one lock to negotiate before reaching the lock to connect with the Don at Stainforth. The land is flat, the line is straight and only the small canal settlements interrupt the route. Thorne has a boatyard of not particularly distinguished architecture, and even that seems overwhelmed by its near neighbours; two railway lines and the M18 all cross nearby. What is remarkable is that it took so long for engineers to appreciate how useful this canal would be – and why did they require three Acts of Parliament in 1793, 1798 and 1809 to raise the money to build it?

At Barnby Dun, the New Junction arrives at an acute angle and on the main line artificial canal gives way to river navigation. Strictly speaking, this does not fall within the scope of this work, but it can hardly be ignored as it is a vital link in the network. The technology has not changed in its essentials, since the early days of river improvements. The haphazard fall of the river is overcome by building weirs across the river, with a cutting to bypass it through a lock. There have been improvements made over the years. The locks are now electrically operated, with movement controlled through lights. Neat not gaudy is the general rule; control cabins are practical, box-like structures with little in the way of decoration. The improvements were made, in large measure, to bring raw materials to the steel works of Rotherham and Sheffield and coal to power stations. Most of the steel industry has gone, power stations have turned away from solid fuels and pit closures have done away with the main cargo anyway. Not so very long ago, Doncaster was one of the busiest spots on the network, sending out coal from a number of surrounding mines. Branches thrust in towards the town centre and wharves and coal chutes are reminders of a busy life. The lock at Doncaster comes as something of a surprise. Suddenly, the whole scale of the canal changes. In 1959, it was entirely rebuilt to a length of 195ft and, as the length of locks on the Sheffield Canal remains unaltered, the explanation has to be found elsewhere, in the Aire & Calder system. Tom Puddings were in regular use on this stretch of canal, but only as far as the New Junction, where they turned off towards Goole.

This waterway is, in general, one which shows its links to industry with often brutal landscapes, but an exception appears beyond Doncaster, heralded by the utilitarian concrete of the A1(M) viaduct. This is a green, deep wooded valley which leads on to Sprotbrough lock and a section where the improvements to navigation are not as obvious as simply increasing lock size. The canalised section has been straightened and in the 1970s Conisbrough lock was removed altogether. It had a rise of just 15in which was compensated for by raising the weir. The brief rural interlude comes to an abrupt

Massive redevelopment of the Manchester Canal docks has produced some interesting new structures, including the Lowry Bridge leading to the Lowry Centre.

end at Conisbrough itself. The most striking feature in the landscape is certainly romantic enough, Conisbrough Castle with its 80ft-high circular keep and immense buttresses. It was built of the local limestone in the late twelfth century, and it is that same stone that has led to the transformation of its surroundings. Huge quarries eat into the hills that border the waterway and provided an important cargo for the Sheffield & South Yorkshire, as the limestone was used as a flux in the iron and steel plants at the end of the line. The railway builders looked elsewhere for their building material when it came to a crossing of the deep Don valley. Conisbrough viaduct consists of a central girder span across the river, approached by fourteen arches at either side and built of hard wearing, blue engineering brick. The bricks have outlived the railway, but that does nothing to diminish the effect. The arches are emphasised by prominent, rounded courses and the whole is topped by a dentilled parapet.

At Swinton, there is a typical modern lock, with its neat cabin, and a junction with the considerably less neat locks that mark the start of the now derelict Dearne & Dove Canal (See Volume 2: *The Mania Years*). Now the industrial world really begins to close in with the approach to the great steel centres of Rotherham and Sheffield. Like so much of Britain's heavy industry one is looking at a working past rather than a thriving present. The modern steel mills are unlovely creations, little more than giant boxes to hold the furnaces and rolling mills, but their sheer size makes them impressive. One of these immense, featureless buildings can be seen close by the

The realignment of the Oxford Canal called for completely new structures, including a new tunnel at Newbold on Avon. With a towpath this tunnel was a great improvement on the old.

waterway, the former Templeborough steel works. The building is over a quarter of a mile long, and 140ft high and now holds the award-winning Magna Science Adventure Centre. Here at least one gets some impression of the industry at its height, for the actual building is still a dark, eerie place, with its spidery network of steel girders and its recreation of the vast E furnace. It is always worth looking at such places, if only to serve as a reminder that even within living memory one of the country's greatest industries was still receiving its raw material by water. As well as the limestone already mentioned, bar iron was imported through Hull, coal came from the surrounding collieries and in its day the whole route was lined with busy staithes.

The concrete viaduct that carries the M1 marks the end of the river navigation and the start of the Sheffield Canal rising up through the eleven Tinsley locks. The old industrial world still exists, but has been overshadowed by the shining green glass of the Meadowhall Centre, and the canal has no place in that world. The customers come to fill the immense car park or arrive on the new light railway system, the modern version of the once despised trams. The canal sees little of the bright new world of Sheffield and a good deal of the grimier side – it is no accident that when film makers wanted a scene to show industrial collapse for *The Full Monty* they chose the canal and its derelict warehouses. The stretch up to Sheffield did not enjoy the benefits of modernisation, and automated locks and traffic lights give way to the more familiar do-it-yourself approach, which means hard work with the heavy gates of the barge locks. But nearing the centre and the end of the line, the canal comes into its own again. As in other cities, its virtues have been recognised and Sheffield Basin has been given the twenty-first-century makeover. It is easy to over romanticise such places. Fred Schofield in his book *Humber Keels and Keelmen* described Sheffield Basin as he remembered it as a boy, arriving on his father's keel in the early years of the twentieth century. It was, he said, a dark, dreary place. 'On the south side a canopy extends out over the basin for the length of four berths, and beyond this is the old warehouse with a waterway right inside; it is impossible to see anything in the cabin without having the lamp burning all the time. On the north side it is more open, but with two coal-burning steam cranes and the steelworks belching out their smoke and soot it is not much brighter.' The steam cranes and steelworks have gone, but it is still possible to recognise the scene described by Fred. The warehouse built out over the water is there, but now holds offices, and behind it is the area that once held the wet dock and the canal company headquarters. All is being redeveloped, but it is too early to say how successful the scheme will prove to be. The main problem appears to be that the basin is a little way out of the city centre, and the location has been made less attractive than it might have been as the busy link road to the M1, the Sheffield Parkway, cuts right across the site. What is here, however, has real

The entrance to Hillmorton maintenance yard, which became the main office for the architecture and planning department of British Waterways. The mellow-brick bridge is itself a constant reminder of traditional values.

73

quality. The main terminal building has a pleasing symmetry. At water level, there is a central segmented arch, with smaller semicircular arches to either side, joined by massive pillars of stone. The arches themselves are lined with stone and have prominent keystones, so that although there is water passing right under the building, it has a reassuringly solid appearance. Above that are three stories, with rows of windows flanking central loading bays. The whole is topped by an attic level and pediment, the slope of the roof emphasised by little semicircular windows at the corners under the eaves and above the central bays. It stands in a cobbled yard, bordered by arches which are also finding new uses. The whole is visually very satisfying, and the quality of the building makes this a canal centre to rank alongside other late flowerings of the canal age such as Ellesmere Port, Gloucester Docks and Sowerby Bridge.

Modernisation was seen by some enterprising companies as the only possible way in which railway competition could be held at bay. Among the engineers who espoused that cause were the Williams family, a father and son both, somewhat confusingly for historians, called Edward Leader Williams. It was to be the son, however, who was to find himself in the position of putting his idea into practice on the grandest scale. The Weaver Navigation enjoyed a busy trade, exporting salt and bringing in raw materials including clay for the potteries. This was a waterway with a long record of improvement, starting with the first Act for making the river navigable, passed in 1720. In 1788 an important decision was taken to build a new dock complex at Anderton, which would act as a trans-shipment point between the Weaver and the Trent & Mersey Canal. The Weaver had its own sailing barges, flats similar to the Mersey flats, considerably larger than the narrow boats of the Trent & Mersey. Movement between the two was at first by hand cart, or by tipping from the canal down to the navigation, not a very satisfactory practice as there was a height difference of 50ft. Throughout the early nineteenth century, the Weaver was being improved. The next decision was to improve access to the waterway by bypassing the awkward tidal waters and creating a new canal and dock complex at Weston Point. The new canal leaves the river above the old Frodsham lock, which originally gave access to the tidal river but then became redundant. It then follows the Weaver valley before turning off to run alongside the coast to the docks and a final lock giving access to the river. In all there were four miles of extra cutting, which included a flood lock at Sutton, now disused. To allow the river craft on to the new section, the bridges had to be made moveable – though the most recent addition, the M56 soars high overhead. This was by no means the end of the improvements. Leader Williams was anxious to introduce steam tugs, and that meant bigger locks. The original eleven locks were reduced to nine, and new locks 100ft long and 22ft wide were introduced from the 1840s onwards. The sensible decision was taken to keep the old 88ft x18ft locks and build the new alongside, so that for all but the largest craft there was now two-way traffic.

One irritating obstacle remained to be dealt with before the new system could be considered really up to date. There was still a considerable amount of trade with the Trent & Mersey, and it was obvious that a better link was needed. There was no question of building locks between the two waterways, draining water away from the upper level which would have to have been replaced by some form of pumping system. Instead Leader Williams designed a vertical lift to be built at Anderton. As described earlier (p.12), it was not the first canal lift but this was built to a far greater scale than its predecessors. The lift was designed with two matched caissons, each 75ft long and 15ft 6in wide and 5ft deep, able to take one flat or a pair of narrow boats. A short aqueduct leads out from the Trent & Mersey to the top of the lift, where gates could be closed off to allow the caissons to move freely as watertight containers. Originally they were counterbalanced and moved using hydraulic power. Considerable ingenuity was needed to provide watertight seals between the aqueduct and the caissons. A timber facing was added to the ends of the aqueduct and the troughs, and a rubber sealant added to the former. The caissons were guided by cast iron blocks running in channels in the fixed structure and each full caisson, weighing some 250 tons was moved by a single hydraulic ram. There were to be changes over the years. The hydraulic system used canal water, which unfortunately was heavily polluted by effluent from surrounding chemical works at Anderton, with the result that it rotted the sealants leading to one catastrophic collapse. An improvement was made by condensing the exhaust steam from auxiliary engines, but a lasting solution arrived in 1902 when hydraulics were abandoned altogether and electric motors installed. Finally, the caisson self-counterbalancing system was scrapped, so that each of the caissons could operate independently. A new counterbalance was supplied by a system of weights dangling in seemingly haphazard fashion around the frame. Recently restored to working condition, the Anderton boat lift is the most impressive example of the Victorian improvements that kept the system in profit. The Weaver continued to thrive even after traditional trades such as salt declined, thanks to the development of the chemical industry, and in time more modern motorised barges took over the traffic.

There were to be more lock enlargements over the years, and for a time the Weaver could boast the largest locks of any British waterway. In the 1870s Leader Williams began the work of constructing locks to the massive dimensions for the time: 220ft x 42ft 6in x 15ft, capable of taking 1000-ton vessels. There was no chance of these being hand operated, so a brand new technology was used. A British mining engineer, Lester Pelton, had discovered that by using high-pressure jets of water impacting on hemispherical cups he could produce a very efficient type of waterwheel. The fall of water at each lock provided a good head, and a pair of Pelton wheels was supplied for each gate. This technology has long since been overtaken, but for those who travel on the Weaver it is worth pausing to consider the engineering ingenuity that went into producing one of the most profitable waterways of its age. It was, however, to be dwarfed by the other great waterway of the nineteenth century, the Manchester Ship Canal.

We know more about the construction of the Manchester Ship Canal than we do about any other of Britain's important waterways. There are two reasons. Firstly it was built in an age which was in love with statistics, and secondly by the time construction started photography was well developed. Work began in 1887, under the direction of the contractor Thomas Walker, who had the hugely ambitious Severn railway tunnel among his impressive list of previous achievements. The technology of the railway age was brought to bear on building the ship canal. There were still vast armies of navvies – at the height of the works over 16,000 men and boys were employed and nearly 200 horses. These would have been impressive figures for any canal of the golden age, but it is the other statistics that set the Ship Canal apart. There were a hundred steam excavators of various kinds and nearly 200 cranes. Spoil was loaded into railway waggons, running on 223 miles of temporary tracks, with an astonishing 173 locomotives for haulage. Add to that hundreds of steam pumps and portable engines and you have a scene where mechanisation has made a huge impact on canal construction for the very first time. The official handbook for 1894 gave figures of 76 million tons of spoil shifted, of which a fifth was rock, while the building materials used included 175,000 cubic yards of brick, 220,000 cubic yards of masonry and, very significantly, 1,250,000 cubic yards of cement. We tend to think of cement as a modern material, and forget that it has been around for a very long time; even the Romans used it for important buildings. Without mechanisation the project could never have been contemplated, let alone completed.

There were five groups of locks, starting with three locks side by side at Eastham, giving access from the Mersey. The other four were built as pairs to economise the use of water. The small locks, and here 'small' is very much a relative term, were 350ft by 45ft, with intermediate gates to allow chambers of 120ft and 230ft to be used. The big locks were 600ft by 65ft, this time with two pairs of intermediate gates. The locks were designed to be operated hydraulically as were the swing bridges that carried roads across the route. In places, the new canal incorporated sections of rivers, including the old Irwell Navigation. The Irwell had been crossed at the very start of the canal age by the Bridgewater Canal via the Barton aqueduct. The latter had to be demolished and a new aqueduct constructed that would not interfere with shipping, and the answer was found with the unique Barton swing aqueduct. Down at Ship Canal level one can still see the stone abutments that brought the old canal towards the river crossing, but now there is an iron trough, 18ft wide and mounted on sturdy iron girders, each 235ft long. The whole structure is carried on roller bearings on a central pier, and the ends of the aqueduct can be closed off by gates held closed by rubber wedges. Once again hydraulic power was used, and the whole structure can be swung, full of water. Very little shipping now uses the canal, so the chances of seeing the structure on the move are slight. It is a pity because it is most impressive, slow and steady and as far as one can see not a drop of water is spilled. It ranks with the Anderton lift as one of the most important structures from the nineteenth-century canal age.

With the opening of the canal, ocean-going ships could now reach to the heart of Manchester, where there was nearly 200 acres of water in the docks and over five miles of quays. The presence of such excellent facilities encouraged local entrepreneurs to develop what can be best described as a forerunner of the modern business park, Trafford Park. It opened for business in 1896 and a number of companies soon moved in. The Co-operative Society established food warehouses,

Hovis built flour mills and Kellogg's began making cornflakes. It was a genuine centre of innovation, and manufacturers at the forefront of development such as British Westinghouse set up works. In the second half of the twentieth century, however, the focus shifted from Manchester to new docks and oil terminals at the Mersey end, as a result of which Ellesmere Port found a new lease of life as a container terminal.

By the 1980s, ship movements on the Manchester end of the canal had all but ceased, and developers began to move in, seeing the old docks as the ideal site for such fashionable concepts as the out-of-town shopping centre. Development around the Manchester and Salford docks has not been the same as in other schemes. Here, much of the old has been completely swept away to make way for the new, rather on the Canary Wharf model. There is, however, an important difference, for Manchester has gone for major public buildings as well as private. The two most important new developments now face each other across the canal, the Lowry Centre and the northern outpost of the Imperial War Museum. The Lowry holds few surprises, but the War Museum is strikingly different. It may not be immediately obvious at first glance, but the building consists of three segments, each supposed to represent the fragments of a globe torn apart by war and the three elements of earth, air and water. There is scarcely a straight line in sight and the whole has something of the look of the rear end of an aircraft. The air segment rears up and is indeed airy and transparent, with its complex steel framework clearly on view. The other elements are lower, gently swelling up from the ground. The architect was Daniel

At Foxton on the Leicester arm of the Grand Union, there was a short-lived attempt to bypass the locks by means of an inclined plane. The track can still be clearly seen and proposals exist for its reconstruction.

Libeskind who also designed the footbridge that curves elegantly across the canal to the Lowry Centre. The engineer was Ove Arup, and like all the bridges on the canal this one is moveable. It will be interesting to see how the Ship Canal develops over the years. At least it has got off to an interesting start.

Improvements and innovations on other canals were not always as dramatic as those on the barge canals. The narrow system of the Midlands was still limited to narrow boat traffic, and there was little or nothing that was going to be done to change that. Improvements were, however, possible and they could be very effective. The Oxford Canal had been built very much in the Brindley tradition and the northern end, above Braunston, was causing severe problems. The development of the system around Birmingham had brought a huge increase in traffic, and if trade was not to be lost something had to be done. In 1828 the company called in the engineer Marc Isambard Brunel, who had already established a considerable reputation after moving to Britain from France, and whose son was to go on to even greater fame. Brunel surveyed the canal and recommended a sensible line for shortening the route. Detailed planning was then passed to Charles Vignoles who presented the completed plans in 1828. Just as Telford had shortened the Birmingham Canal by cutting a new main line straight through the meanders of the old, so now the same was to be done on the Oxford Canal, shortening the route by nearly fourteen miles, which meant in effect all but halving it. Other improvements included doubling up the locks and replacing the old, narrow tunnel at Newbold with a broad, new tunnel, able to pass two boats at a time and equipped with the luxury of towpaths to either side.

The improvements were not perhaps all that they might have been. Two locks side by side were an improvement on a single lock, but an even better answer would have been to build wide locks instead. This would have been particularly useful once motor boats came onto the canal. As it was, the motor had to go in first and the butty was then hauled in afterwards, instead of being able to sit snugly side by side. Steps were, however, taken to ensure that there was enough water to keep two locks at work. A steam engine was installed behind the workshops at Hillmorton to supply the pound above the three double locks. Hillmorton itself has its own special place in this story. The maintenance yard here is not unlike many another on the waterways system, a place of plain, no-nonsense buildings. It is approached via a somewhat awkward turn under a mellow brick bridge, which itself carries one clue as to why the whole seems so satisfying. The bricks are, unlike modern machine-made bricks, hand made; they were fired in ill-regulated kilns so there is no colour uniformity. They might be called red bricks, but the name 'red' covers a variety of shades from something verging on pink to a deep hue that is almost purple. The result is a subtle blending of colours that gives a rich patina to the whole. And what is true of the bridge is true of the other buildings in the complex. The other feature that is instantly apparent is that sense of proportion coupled with a simple rhythmic pattern of arched windows on the main buildings. These visual pleasures have been commented on before, but it is still easy to forget how very simple it would be to modernise such buildings, replacing cast-iron window lights by more durable plastic for example. That this has not been done throughout Britain's canal system is due in no small part to the team that now works in the offices here. In 1970 British Waterways Board appointed its first architect, Peter White, and Hillmorton was to become his headquarters. There are architects who will always be remembered for the great buildings that they designed. Peter will, I know, not mind if I say that he is not one of that select group. But what everyone who cares about canals should thank him for is his crucial role as a conservationist. He has never been one of those who have said that all that is old is good, and all that is new is bad, but he has always been absolutely convinced that the canals spoke of their own time and that they had a unique character that needed to be preserved. Whatever new that was added should take cognisance of that fact. He did not win every battle, but he won a great many, and if today that essential character has been preserved then it is due in no small part to Peter's work and those who have followed on after his retirement. It is a subject that will be looked at in more detail later in the book. As in Birmingham, the old loops survived – if only for a time – and the towpath of the new cut was carried over these by Horseley Iron Works bridges.

Not every canal modernisation programme proved a success. A long-standing cause of delays on the Leicester Arm of the Grand Union was caused by the Foxton staircase locks, which could take well over an hour for a boat to pass through. A proposed solution was an inclined plane. In 1896 a complete working model was constructed at the Bulbourne yard, and when that proved successful, work began at Foxton. The system worked by floating a pair of narrow boats into one of the two caissons, which acted to counterbalance one another. Power was supplied by a small steam engine. The caissons were each 80ft long by 15ft wide and ran on a concrete ramp. There were eight sets of wheels, arranged in four pairs and mounted on a triangular frame set at the same angle as the incline, so that the caissons themselves remained horizontal. The ramp was set with eight rails for each caisson. It achieved its aim, taking just twelve minutes to move boats through a vertical lift of 80ft. It was opened in 1900 and although it was successful in shortening journey times, it proved expensive to run. The engine had to be kept in steam even when not needed, and there was none of the anticipated increase in traffic. In 1926, the incline was closed. It had cost nearly £40,000 to build and the machinery was sold off for a mere £250. The cutting to the incline is still there, the ramp has recently been cleared and there are ambitious plans for restoration. It remains, however, as a reminder that while many expensive modernisation programmes proved well worth the time and effort expended, this was not always the case.

5. North of the Border

Readers who have seen Volume 1 of this series may remember that, at the time it was written, the publishers had been planning a separate volume covering Scotland. As a result, the first of the Scottish canals was omitted. As it turned out, that was fortunate because in the intervening period a great deal has happened. For a start, the Forth & Clyde Canal has been completely restored and reopened and can finally be given the treatment it deserves.

The notion of a canal that would unite the two great rivers had been around for some time before definite moves were made to obtain an Act of Parliament. The impetus came, as it did for other canals of the period, from the success of the Bridgewater Canal. Even so, first attempts were unsuccessful, largely because the gentlemen of Edinburgh were at odds with those of Glasgow. Many Scots would argue that they still are. However, in 1768 the Act was duly obtained and the post of engineer went to John Smeaton. He is perhaps best known for his daring work in building the Eddystone lighthouse, but he had already worked as engineer on the Calder & Hebble navigation in Yorkshire. The 1760s have become known as the age of Brindley, but here was a man, one of the founding fathers of the profession of civil engineer, who was to work in a very different way. It was decided from the first that this was to be a ship canal albeit one of modest dimensions, able to take vessels 69ft by 19ft. This was not a canal to be cut through a gentle countryside, but one which had to climb to a height of over 150ft above sea level. What Brindley would have made of it, one can only guess, but Smeaton showed himself to be a master of surveying and planning. There were to be twenty locks from the Forth to the summit, which was to be sixteen miles long, and a further nineteen locks down to the Clyde. Because it was intended for use by masted ships all the bridges had to be moveable, and there was one immense aqueduct as well as several smaller ones. The summit was to be supplied by reservoirs. There were numerous delays during construction, and the work passed from Smeaton to Robert MacKell in 1773. He stayed on the project for six years before the money ran out and everything was stopped again. It was at last completed in 1785 under a third engineer, Robert Whitworth. He celebrated the event by carrying a symbolic bottle of water from the Forth along the canal and emptying it into the Clyde. The line, however, was Smeaton's and a very direct line it was too, running from an entrance lock at Grangemouth in the east to Bowling in the west, a distance of thirty-five miles.

The canal was closed in 1962, although it still had a not inconsiderable traffic, not just pleasure boats but fishing boats and even the occasional cargo vessel. Suspicion at the time fell on a new bypass. If the canal was to be kept open, it would have had to have included an expensive lifting bridge, and even if the expense had been met nobody was keen on traffic being held up on a busy road to allow a boat down the old canal. Over the years, the locks lost their gates, bridges were dropped and sections culverted. The only meaningful survivor was the basin at Bowling on the Clyde, which proved a useful haven, particularly for yachts. It was only at the end of the last century that canal restoration moved away from the era of beery, bearded amateurs – rather to the regret of some of us – and into a more professional world. Big money suddenly became available so that work could be contracted out to professional engineers and builders. Now, the canal has reopened, and what we see today is a mixture of the old and the new. Replacement bridges are no longer moveable, because it is no longer seen as a route for any vessels that cannot pass under a normal bridge. The new approach is typified by the solution to one of the biggest problems confronting the restorers. The canal was blocked off by the busy dual carriageway, carrying the A80, the main road from Glasgow to Stirling. There was absolutely no way that any form of lifting or swing bridge could be built on this busy road, so height had to be sacrificed. The age when vessels with tall masts could use the canal was over. It was the price that had to be paid for reopening. So, the A80 crosses the canal on what can only be described as a concrete slab. However, even allowing for the loss in height, there were still problems to be overcome, and one of the most troublesome was at Dalmuir, where the canal is crossed by the main road from Glasgow to Dumbarton. There was no question of replacing the low bridge in

The start of the Forth & Clyde Canal, looking out from the entrance lock at Bowling Basin to the broad waters of the Clyde. The size of the lock indicates that this canal was intended for sea-going vessels.

Kelvin aqueduct is carried on stone piers with prominent cutwaters. The shape is carried right up to the parapet, giving it an odd, scalloped appearance.

Spiers Wharf, Glasgow, is one of the most imposing examples of early canalside development in Britain. The buildings include warehouses, stables and a classical pedimented office.

The former bonded warehouse of the Rosebank distillery, Falkirk, retains something of its fortress-like appearance; today, however, the owners hope to lure the drinkers in, rather than keep them out.

It would be easy to imagine that one was looking at a pair of railway viaducts, but the nearer of the two structures is the Slateford aqueduct, betrayed by the railings.

a built up area. So, if the bridge was not to go up, then the canal would have to go down. A drop lock, the only one of its kind in Europe, was built. Boats enter the lock, the water level is reduced, they go under the bridge, and the water level is raised again. Smeaton, who was fascinated by water power and water movement, would, one feels, have rather enjoyed it. What he would have thought of another innovation, is more difficult to guess. We have all got used to the American import, the drive-through hamburger takeaway. But is there anywhere else that can match the Forth & Clyde's sail-through fish and chip shop?

This description starts at Bowling, where many original features have survived. The basin is approached through the sea lock, giving access to the tidal Clyde. At such an important terminus there is a suitably grand office, at least in terms of size. It stands two storeys high, but has dormers in the roof, indicating attic space, and has a two-storey hipped roof extension at the back. The first bridge along the way carries the Glasgow to Dumbarton railway and was built while the canal was still in regular use, so it had to be moveable, the central girder section sliding on rollers mounted on stone piers. That leads on to the first of the locks and the first of the bascule bridges. These latter structures have an ingenious method for lifting the platform. What appears at first to be a semicircular metal hoop at the end of the bridge is actually two quadrants geared together. The pinion on the inside of the fixed quadrant engages with a spur wheel on the inner rim of the other, and movement comes through gears operated by a simple cranked winding handle. Movement is

The Almond aqueduct is a very self-assured structure. The splayed piers have a reassuring solidity.

The neat stables by the canal at Linlithgow are now home to a canal museum, which continues a strong tradition of running steam boats for passengers to enjoy the waterway.

eased by counterweights in pits sunk into the bridge abutments. Originally the canal had both single and double leaf bridges. For reasons which are not altogether clear, the lifting mechanism for double leaf bridges was not necessarily the same at the two ends, though they work on the same principle. One new swing bridge has been built, though it is overshadowed by the huge and elegant Erskine Bridge that crosses the canal at lock 37 on its way over the far wider waters of the Clyde.

The canal passes round the northern outskirts of Glasgow, climbing steadily. The most interesting section is the flight of five locks at Maryhill, separated by oval pounds to ensure a good water supply. The other notable feature on this section is the Kelvin aqueduct. This was the work of Robert Whitworth and was completed in 1790. It crosses the river on four stone semicircular arches, with prominent cutwaters in between. The line of the cutwaters is carried up to the parapet, resulting in an unusual scalloped shape, when seen in plan. A little way past the aqueduct is a junction with a branch leading down to Port Dundas and the Monkland Canal, which served local iron foundries. Port Dundas was the canal showcase. Here the company built their magnificent classical office around 1812. The building has a pedimented central bay, with a porched entrance and a roundel decoration. The bays to either side end in pilasters. It would be quite acceptable as a grand country house. Sadly, Port Dundas has been separated from the rest of the system by the building of the M8. Fortunately, however, the Spiers Wharf area has survived as part of the restoration programme. Here is an impressive range of warehouses, cobbled quays and stables. The stables were a standard design for the canal, and look surprisingly similar to the canal offices at Port Dundas. Once again, there is a two-storey main block, but with a central advanced bay with a pediment. It seems extraordinary that such architectural elegance should be devoted to canal horses, but it has encouraged developers to find new uses for the buidings. At Kirkintilloch, they have been converted into a pub and restaurant.

The line to the east of the junction with the Glasgow branch is all the work of Smeaton. At Kirkintilloch there is a small aqueduct over Luggie Water. This is a simple structure, carried on a single semicircular arch, not as grand as the Kelvin aqueduct, but nevertheless it has an elegance which was rarely found on English aqueducts of the same period. It is reassuringly solid, built of large stone blocks to carry the trough with its dense layer of puddled clay. Decoration is sparse but effective, including a dentilled parapet running between stone columns that stand at each side of the wide arch. The section through Kirkintilloch runs along the course of an earlier engineering marvel, the Antonine Wall. One section here is tree lined, so that it looks very much as if a canal has strayed across the Channel from France. Smeaton encountered one major problem to the east of Kirkintilloch, an area of marshland known as the Dullatur Bog. His solution was that adopted by other early

The Union Canal served a busy, industrial world and there are still reminders of old industries. Here the canal runs past 'the bings' left over from the shale oil extraction industry.

The tiny lock cottage at Falkirk is built in the Scottish vernacular, and shows the traditional decoration of outlining window and door surrounds.

canal engineers. He kept piling on earth until he had a stable embankment, then he cut his canal, broad, straight and true across the morass.

The descent down to the Forth begins shortly after the long straight. There is a curious little aqueduct at Bonnybridge, not odd in itself for it is quite a minor structure, but the burn it crosses has a footpath alongside, so that those who walk this way appear to be going through a tunnel. The canal attracted industries to its banks, including that most Scottish of all industries, the whisky distillery. The Rosebank distillery was established in the 1790s, and the most interesting building is a bonded warehouse, built as a wedge to fit the site between road and canal. It has a rounded end which provides a note of grace in what would otherwise be a somewhat grim structure. Bonded warehouses tend to look like prisons, with small, barred windows. Here, however, the object is not to keep criminals in, but to keep them out. Falkirk also provided the canal with one of its most important customers, the world famous Carron ironworks, who regularly shipped their wares down to Glasgow and had their own warehouse at Port Dundas. Now it was just a short run down to the Forth at Grangemouth. This end of the route has been built over, so a new terminal has been created with the navigable River Carron.

The Forth & Clyde was always an innovative company. They were the first to experiment with steam, but although the experiment was a success, they declined to use steam tugs at first as they feared the effect of the wash on the banks. As early as 1783, they began a passenger service, using a barge with cabins at either end, one for ladies and the other for gentlemen. This was so successful that in 1809 they began a daily service of passenger boats, offering a very comfortable journey with two classes of cabins and meals on board. The boats were pulled by two horses, one of which was ridden, and the best runs finished the journey between Falkirk and Glasgow in three hours. Horses were changed at regular intervals, and it was for this service that the stable blocks were built. It was money well spent, for the numbers travelling by canal reached 44,000 in 1812. This was one of the factors that encouraged entrepreneurs to push for a new canal that would provide a direct link between Glasgow and the capital, Edinburgh. One reminder of the success of that scheme can be seen at the junction where the two canals were eventually to meet. The Union Inn was built to house passengers waiting to transfer between boats. The popularity of the canal was continued on the Forth & Clyde in the nineteenth century by pleasure steamers, known as the Queens.

Work on the Edinburgh & Glasgow Union, generally known as the Union Canal, began in 1817. Telford was called in as a consultant in the early stages but the main work went to Hugh Baird as chief engineer.

The design of the canal was exceptionally bold. A flight of eleven locks led up from the Forth & Clyde to the new canal, and once the climb was completed the Union remained on a level all the way to a terminus half a mile from Edinburgh

The restoration of the Union Canal involved new engineering works, which included constructing a tunnel under the railway. The result is drab but practical.

castle. This was not achieved without considerable engineering works, which included three major aqueducts and what was at the time Scotland's only canal tunnel. There was one problem, however, that did not arise. The new canal was not a ship canal, but intended only for use by barges, so conventional, fixed bridges could be used.

The timing of the canal seemed propitious, for it opened in 1822 at just the period when Edinburgh New Town was being developed, so that there was an immediate demand for building stone and slate. The passenger service continued to thrive, but only until 1842 when the Edinburgh & Glasgow Railway was opened. A familiar story now followed of declining traffic and railway take over, a process which culminated in the closure and destruction of the locks in 1933, cutting the connection to the Forth & Clyde. The rest of the waterway remained more or less open, though a chunk of valuable land was reclaimed for building at the Edinburgh end. Some thirty miles still remained in water, though over the years obstructions appeared as sections were filled in, culverted and had low road bridges built over them to block the line. However, the main structures, such as the aqueducts, remained and restoration is now nearly complete. The following description will certainly be out of date by the time it is read, and it may well be that the remaining obstacles will all have been removed. The canal starts now with a basin in the Fountainbridge district of Edinburgh, less than half a mile from Princes Street. When I visited the site, the basin was divorced from the system by the comparatively modern Lemington lift bridge. This is an unusual structure, in that the whole road platform is raised vertically through overhead pulleys on an ungainly metal gantry. The movement is counterbalanced by weights, out of sight within the supporting framework. The deck has latticed rails at the side, and the same design is repeated on the nearby pedestrian footbridge. At the time it remained immobile, and the road authorities would probably have liked it to remain that way. But agreement was eventually reached to restore it to working order, and by May 2002 the bridge was moving again. After that initial stutter, the canal makes its way through the suburbs, passing under the first of the original stone bridges. The basic structure is similar to that of the other stone bridges, with a segmented arch and the number on the prominent keystone. However, it acknowledges its importance as Number 1, by having a stepped parapet above the abutments and by having the Edinburgh coat of arms carved on its eastern side and the Glasgow arms on the other. The attractive effect is rounded off by neat iron railings running between pillars on each side of the arch. The canal now leads on to Harrison Park, where a new boathouse has recently been built. It has something of a jaunty, Edwardian air about it, with a very open frame, verandah and a neat little cupola. The surroundings remain urban, with new housing now lining the bank. There follows an interesting contrast in styles. At Slateford, the canal crosses the Slateford Road on a 1937 concrete aqueduct. Its style is reminiscent of the aqueducts of a similar date on the Birmingham Canal, with the trough connected to the supporting arches by vertical columns. It is immediately followed by the original Slateford aqueduct built to cross the Water of Leith. Its outward appearance suggests a conventional stone

The aqueduct leading out to the top of the Falkirk Wheel.

aqueduct, 500ft long, built on eight tapering piers linked by semicircular arches. The piers are wider than the arch, and they are continued upwards to appear above the parapet, where they are linked by iron railings. The effect is very striking, emphasising the height of the whole structure. It is not as solid as it appears. The actual trough is cast iron, so is comparatively light, and as a result the piers themselves are hollow. The same system was used on the other two big nineteenth-century aqueducts on the canal.

There were many obstructions to overcome in the next few miles, and removing them produced one or two surprises. The Dumbryden Road Bridge had been covered over when an embankment was constructed above it in the 1970s. When the earthworks had been removed, the bridge re-emerged not much the worse for wear, and only required a little patching to bring it back into use. Other bridges have been replaced by utilitarian concrete. A more difficult problem arose when construction began on the Edinburgh bypass. The road builders, not altogether unreasonably, wanted to keep construction as simple as possible, which would have meant building the road straight across the canal at water level. The canal interest prevailed, the road dips and the canal crosses it on a brand new concrete aqueduct. It is carried on pillars with curved ends, two to either side of the road, and the third in the centre of the dual carriageway. It is a good example of turning what could have been a set of dull, angular slabs into something altogether more appealing with very little trouble.

The canal emerges from the outskirts of Edinburgh, though not into an entirely peaceful countryside thanks to the close attention of the M8, said to be Scotland's busiest road. Ratho was one of the more important canal settlements and the canal inn still stands beside one of the well preserved original bridges. That is followed by, not the grandest, but the most attractive of the big three aqueducts, across the wooded valley of the River Almond. In style it is identical to the Slateford aqueduct. Here there are just five arches, the three central ones being the tallest and crossing the river itself. The main water supply for the canal comes in through a feeder at the eastern end from the Cobbinslaw reservoir. The canal finally crosses the motorway and turns north, through a rather eerie landscape towards Winchburgh. The village itself was built from 1901 onwards by the Winchburgh Oil Co., formed to extract oil from shale. The spoil was heaped in immense flat-topped waste heaps, known as 'shale bings' beside the canal. This gives way to a tree-shaded cutting.

For a canal that remains on the level, the Union has no shortage of points of interest. There is one other major aqueduct across the River Avon, the longest and the tallest of the three, 800ft long and 80ft high, with twelve arches. Linlithgow is the most important stopping place reached so far, and the stables by Manse Road Basin have now been converted into a canal museum, and used as a centre for trip boats. These buildings are far more utilitarian than the immense mansion-like stables on the Forth & Clyde. The single storey block has five arched openings giving direct access to the wharf. The road access to the wharf still has its gate houses in place, making this an unusually complete site. Slightly grander two-storey stables can be seen at Woodcockdale. The canal now heads off towards Falkirk and more heavy engineering. A deep cutting is crossed by the high 'laughin' and greetin'' bridge. The keystones have carvings, with a cheerful face on one side and a solemn, not to say glum, on the other. Tradition has it that two contractors took work on this stretch of the canal; one made a profit, the other went bankrupt. The cutting ends at the 696 yard long Falkirk tunnel. Again, there is a popular story that the wealthy owners of Callendar Park insisted that the canal was tucked away out of sight. There are several objections to the story. In the first place, Falkirk was already a heavily industrialised town by the time the canal was built, and the landscape itself demanded either a long detour or an unreasonably deep cutting. The tunnel was a logical choice.

Now the canal arrives at the top of the former locks, and nowhere in the story of canal restoration in the past fifty years have engineers been so bold as they have here. The first obstacle to a reunion with the Forth & Clyde was the Glasgow to Edinburgh main line, and the canal was dropped down and sent underneath it, giving Scotland its second canal tunnel. Then the real challenge came, the gap once occupied by eleven locks. The solution was the Falkirk Wheel. A row of tall, concrete hoops on stilts, like overgrown needles was built out from the hillside to a point above a new basin on the Forth & Clyde. An aqueduct was carried on this unusual structure to the wheel itself. In essence, the idea is not new. This is a boat lift, with two counterbalanced caissons. But instead of moving vertically as in all previous boat lifts, these are set within the wheel, diametrically opposite each other.

Boats going downhill pass through a watertight gate which is closed behind them, and similarly boats can enter the lower caisson at the same time. Then the wheel begins to turn. Each caisson has a wheeled bogie running inside the ring, automatically finding the lowest level through gravity, so that the caisson always remains level and no water is spilled. After half a revolution of the wheel, the bottom caisson is now at the top and vice versa. This giant structure of concrete and steel stands 115ft high and manages what all the greatest canal structures have achieved. It combines elegance of operation with an equally elegant appearance. The steel wheel itself was manufactured at the Butterley works in Derbyshire, which adds a delightful note of continuity, since this was the works founded by William Jessop and Benjamin Outram. To add a further note of historical serendipity, Outram was among the pioneers in the use of iron on the waterways, when he designed the cast iron aqueduct at Derby at about the same time that Telford was making his experiments in Shropshire. At the foot of the wheel is a large basin, and beyond that the Forth & Clyde. After seventy years of separate existence, the two canals have finally been reunited. The Falkirk Wheel represents one aspect of restoration. In many cases, what has been needed was a refurbishment of the old, the restoration of the historic canal landscape. Here is the exact opposite, a modern solution of great ingenuity which has already been added to the list of the great and inspiring structures of the past.

Not all Scottish canals have shared the good fortune of the two described above. Early in the nineteenth century two waterways schemes were going forward at the same time, and nobody seemed to have noticed that they were incompatible. One was for the improvement of the navigation of the Clyde. It seems remarkable now that the river which has seen the birth of some of the world's greatest ships was once so shallow in Glasgow that it was possible to ford it to avoid paying tolls on the bridge. The solution was to turn the river into a giant canal by building jetties out from the banks and joining these by a continuous wall. Not everyone was convinced. The Earl of Eglinton thought that a much better solution would be a new canal running south west from Glasgow to Ardrossan, where a whole new port would be created. In 1806, the Act was passed for the construction of the Glasgow, Paisley & Ardrossan Canal and work got under way at much the same time as it did on the Clyde. Thomas Telford, inevitably, was involved in both schemes, as he was in virtually all engineering works in Scotland in the early nineteenth century. Unfortunately for the canal fraternity, the Clyde scheme proved wholly successful. The canal had reached as far as Johnstone, just beyond Paisley when all work came to a halt. The effort, however, proved not to be entirely wasted. In 1881 the company was bought out by the Glasgow & South Western Railway. The canal was drained and a railway built on top of it. How many people realise that the bridge carrying the railway over the White Cart Water between Glasgow and Paisley started its working life as a canal aqueduct?

6. The Restoration Years

It is easy to lose sight of the fact that many of the canals that we travel for pleasure today have gone through a transformation from busy commercial waterways, through a period of decay and dereliction to rebirth as leisure routes. Popular features such as the various rings, offering a chance of a holiday cruise which takes one round a whole circuit, and returns to the start, would not have been possible without the restoration movement's efforts. The Cheshire Ring for example would not exist without the restored Ashton, Peak Forest and Rochdale Canals. Whether dashing around a ring at speed to get back by a prescribed time is the ideal way to travel canals or not is a quite different matter. The fact remains that rings such as this are popular and well used, and even those who choose to travel using different criteria can join in with thanks that such wonderful waterways as the Peak Forest are again navigable. But the question is increasingly asked: what do we mean by restoration? Should it involve no more than the careful recreation of what has gone before, or should we be looking for new solutions, using new materials? Throughout this work, the emphasis has been on the way in which the canals were built in the late eighteenth and early nineteenth centuries as parts of an industrial world. The engineers used the latest technology available to them at the time and the most appropriate and, often the cheapest, materials that were to be found close to the site. They designed their canals to meet quite specific needs, to provide the most up to date and efficient transport system for a developing industrial world. Canals no longer serve that world, nor are they an efficient form of transport if one takes all costs into consideration. True, moving goods by water is very energy efficient, but it is slow and when factors such as working hours are put into the equation, the economic arguments look less secure. This is especially true of the narrow canals. Again one forgets what a leap forward they were in the mid-eighteenth century. There was no such thing as rapid bulk transport, so the labour costs were very little different for a man driving a cart pulled by a horse from those with one steering a boat pulled by a similar animal. But the man on the boat could shift perhaps fifty times as much per journey as the man with the cart. This was not just an improvement, this was an immense leap, a genuine transport revolution. No one can blame those men who, in the 1760s, decided that narrow canals would be perfectly adequate for the country's needs. The improvement they were offering was so massive anyway that no one was concerned that it might be made even better. But then no one was imagining the arrival of the steam locomotive, let alone the internal combustion engine. I have long since lost track of the number of times I have been asked the question: 'Wouldn't it be a good idea to take goods off the road and bring the canals back into use?' I am expected to agree wholeheartedly that it would be a good idea, and I am very happy to agree that some

The new Telford main line of the Birmingham Canal heads straight for its destination. It has cut across the original Brindley line, which has been preserved here as the Soho Loop, turning off under the Horseley iron bridge.

The Engine Arm aqueduct crossing the main line of the Birmingham Canal. Telford had, by this date, started taking an interest in the increasingly popular Gothic style, so he added pointed arches and quatrefoils to his design.

waterways, notably those of north-east England, should be more widely used. That is not the same thing as arguing that all canals should turn to freight. This was an argument that caused a great deal of friction and even downright animosity at the beginning of the restoration movement. It is necessary to go back to that time, because decisions taken then have had a profound effect on the landscape of canals today. Imagine for a moment, if there had been a huge investment in waterways as modern transport systems for cargo, bringing the narrow canals up to the standard of, for example, the Aire & Calder. Would they look anything like they do now? They certainly would not. Would a leisure industry have developed that has been so successful that current worries are being expressed not on where the traffic on canals will be found, but over whether it is already so great as to be straining the system? That too seems equally unlikely. We can look back on the early years to see who won the arguments of freight against leisure, restoration versus replacement, and who lost.

It is not very often that a single book can be said to have had a profound effect on the world outside of literature and the arts, but L.T.C. Rolt's masterpiece *Narrow Boat* did just that. It described a journey by canal taken at the very beginning of the Second World War. It looked at a way of life which was slipping away, but which Rolt saw as valuable in itself, and as having its roots in a great, old tradition. In his words: 'The factories and mean streets of our industrial cities may represent the

At Galton Bridge, Telford reverted to a straightforward design, and this graceful arch is in no need of embellishment.

Brindley Place is perhaps the most startling transformation scene on the Birmingham system and has proved hugely successful. All that remains of the old is the Broad Street bridge in the background.

wealth of England, but the greatness of the English tradition was born of our fields and villages, and is dying with the peasant, the yeoman and the craftsman.' He saw the canals and the families who worked on them as part of the latter rural tradition, and he saw that when the war was over that way of life would be under threat. Near the end of the book, he wrote: 'But if the canals are left to the mercies of economists and scientific planners, before many years are past the last of them will become a weedy, stagnant ditch, and the bright boats will rot at the wharves, to live only in old men's memories.' With Britain at war, nothing could be done, but in 1946 the whole question of the future of the canal system came under review.

Rolt was by then established as a prominent figure in the canal world, and was invited to present his views in a discussion paper for the Association for Planning and Regional Reconstruction. It was an invitation not without its irony since this was precisely the sort of body he had prophesied as turning into agents of doom. He was concerned about the marginal waterways, such as the Kennet & Avon, writing very sensibly that 'it is far easier and cheaper to maintain a waterway in navigable condition than it is to restore it to such a condition after it has been abandoned'. How many tens and even hundreds of millions might have been saved in the past half century if anyone had paid attention to that sound advice! Rolt had a very personal view of the canals which was tied to his vision of an old tradition opposed to the brutalities of industrialisation. Much as I have always admired Rolt and his work, this is a view I cannot accept. Canals were built to serve an industrial world: that was the only reason they were built. The fact that they no longer seemed relevant to the industrial world of the mid–twentieth century was no more than historical movement, the inevitable creation of new transport systems. If the early generation had had access to mechanical diggers, concrete for construction and motors for their boats they would have used them all. The canal world they would have created would have been very different, and a good deal less appealing. Making attractive structures came as a natural result of the adoption of traditional materials and vernacular styles, but though the most important structures might be given an appropriately grand form of decoration, aesthetics was never high on the agenda. This argument about different ways of looking at the canal system was to dominate the early years of restoration.

Rolt's work had not gone unnoticed. The author and critic Robert Aickman had developed an enthusiasm for canals, and he invited Rolt and other interested parties to a meeting at his London house in 1946. Charles Hadfield, who had yet to make his name as Britain's leading canal historian, was there, as was Frank Eyre who had come at Charles's invitation. The result of the meeting was the formation of a canal pressure group, the Inland Waterways Association (IWA), with Aickman as chairman, Hadfield as vice chairman, Rolt as secretary and Eyre as treasurer. The group was never in total agreement, and there were personality clashes from the start. Rolt's position was clear: he was primarily concerned to bring the canals back to life as working waterways. Hadfield shared his new friend's enthusiasm for the working life of the waterways but had grave doubts whether cargo carrying could survive throughout the system. He saw a split in the canal world as the only answer:

encouraging freight on the broad, modern waterways and developing the narrow canals for leisure. Rolt wanted all the efforts to be concentrated on the canals still carrying working boats: Aickman wanted no limits set. His primary concern was with the leisure industry that he saw as being the main hope for the survival of canals in the future. Charles Hadfield, with a living to earn, joined the Civil Service, and concentrated on researching the history of canals. He did not get on with Aickman, to put it at its mildest. Rolt found the demands being made on his time increasingly difficult to reconcile with the rest of his life, for he too had to earn a living. He was also increasingly at odds with Aickman about the direction in which the infant IWA was moving. It seems extraordinary today that an honest difference of opinion should be treated rather like a proposal to massacre the innocents. The split when it came was bitter and acrimonious. Charles Hadfield was asked to recant his heresies or resign. He declined to do either, and his subscription was returned and he was ousted. At the very first IWA rally, Rolt was advised that if he turned up with his famous narrow boat *Cressy*, which had begun it all, he would not be welcomed. It was to be the end of his active involvement with the IWA and the restoration movement set off on a course charted increasingly by Robert Aickman. Two of the founding figures, the man who had inspired it all and the other who was to set canal history onto a sound footing, were no longer welcome. Not everyone was happy with the way things were going, and some restoration groups, notably the Kennet & Avon, broke away to form their own canal organisations. The main proponents of the canal are all dead, and the arguments are now rehearsed in histories and memoirs, not in practice. It does, however, seem to be relevant to understand that restoration seemed neither obviously desirable in all cases, nor was the question of how restoration should proceed at all clear. We have the benefit of hindsight; we know how that story ends. Canal restoration is all about canals for leisure. A system built for the hard-nosed world of commerce is being transformed for holiday making. The key questions now are: how much of the old needs to be saved, and how do we incorporate the new? The answers were not immediately obvious half a century ago.

The idea of using canals for pleasure was not entirely new. Passenger boats had been an important part of the canal scene from the beginning, but in those days they were seen as a convenient and speedy way of travelling around the country. There were some, even then, who also found the notion of canal travel rather attractive – so long as the canal was in the country, not in the town. Sir George Head gave his views of travel on the Bridgewater Canal packet boat in the nineteenth century:

> This mode of travelling, to an easy-going individual, provided it be not repeated too often, is far from disagreeable: – there he sits without troubling himself with the world's concerns, basking in the sunshine, and gliding through a continuous panorama of cows, cottages, and green fields, the latter gaily sparkling in the season with buttercups and daisies ... It is true there is one drawback to the comfort of the traveller, – namely, that within a dozen miles of Manchester the water of the canal is as black as the Styx, and absolutely pestiferous, from the gas and refuse of the many factories with which it is impregnated.

Old Turn Junction is a good example of how old and new can blend successfully together. It is interesting to note just how modern the original iron bridge looks, proving that good design never dates.

The area around Farmers Bridge was one of the first to be developed, with the Indoor Arena taking full advantage of its waterside site.

This is a view of canal travel which, with some variations, has lasted down the years. Early canal guides tended to be spattered with remarks such as 'unfortunately the canal now reaches an industrial region', conveniently forgetting why canals were built. Sir George was travelling on a regular passenger service, but by the end of the nineteenth century people were taking boats for pleasure trips on the canals. A magazine article of 1885 mentioned a barge on the Regent's Canal with a sign advertising 'boats to let for school and picnic parties'. There were even intrepid parties hiring narrow boats for holidays, though they called them barges and in an 1891 account by V. Cecil Cotes called *Two Girls on a Barge*, the author also described their working companions as 'Mr Bargee and Mrs Bargee'. The girls also set about transforming the working boat by having the hold scrubbed out and partitioned into temporary cabins. There was no question of enjoying an 'authentic' experience of canal travel – all the hard work could safely be left to Mr and Mrs Bargee. The boat was to become a drawing room on water. 'There were curtains to hang. Liberty curtains that had taken a whole day to choose, and "dhurries" to be draped over the fresh-scented pine of the little cabins; and Liberty again in innumerable hangings to be arranged all around the bulwarks gracefully.'

This is the background against which the modern restoration movement has to be seen, the context in which decisions were taken. Were the canals to try and preserve the working life, or if that was not possible should they at least remain honest to its memories? Or were canals to be thought of as simply elongated boating parks, there to give pleasure? If the former was to be important, then urban as well as rural canals would have their place and historical structures would be respected. If the latter, then towns, or at any rate industrial towns, could simply be ignored and the emphasis could safely be left on drifting through flowery meadows while the chintz curtains flapped at the windows. In the event, the result has been something of a compromise, following an old British tradition.

There are many places around the canal system where one can see that restoration has involved a deliberate decision to recreate the historic landscape, while at the same time new structures have been introduced to meet modern needs. A very good example is the Kennet Navigation, already described in some detail in Volume 1, but it is worth looking at just one spot to see the two approaches side by side. At Aldermaston, the old lock was in a bad state of repair when the restorers came along, while right below it the way was blocked by what had been a swing bridge but had now become permanently fixed. The lock was to become something of a showcase for the canal. Its side walls consist of rows of shallow brick arches, so that it appears to have scalloped edges, but it was all in very poor condition. The simple solution would have been to create a conventional lock chamber, but instead the old bricks were renewed and new neat brick copings added. The surrounds were also bricked. Under the arc of the balance beams are heel grips consisting of engineering bricks set on edge to provide purchase for boaters pushing against the beams. Bollards are neat and functional, and there is a happy little nod at history in the guard rails, set back from the edge of the lock. The canal was once in the ownership of the Great Western Railway, and old GWR rails have been used for the job. The whole effect is visually very pleasing, a good example of how a unique type of lock has been preserved without in any way reducing its usability.

Swing bridges are very much a feature of the Kennet Navigation, but are an obvious inconvenience to motorists. There was strong opposition to unblocking the bridge at Aldermaston. It was clear that simply restoring the old hand-operated swing bridge was not an option. Equally building a new fixed bridge presented practical problems. For the road to be raised high enough to allow boats to pass underneath it would have been necessary to build approach ramps. This might have been possible in open country, but here there are houses alongside the road. The answer was to construct a lift bridge. There is no tradition of lift bridges on the waterway, so the sensible thing was to start from scratch and design a wholly modern structure. So what we have today is a steel platform, raised by hydraulic rams. It is not particularly attractive, but it works – and without a practical, modern bridge such as this the canal would have remained blocked. So here we have the two aspects of restoration: preservation of the old, solving the problems created by changes in the modern world.

The example of Aldermaston seems to me to be a triumph of common sense, but are both approaches needed? Some would argue that the only thing that really matters is getting the waterway open. Why should one be concerned with the work of eighteenth-century engineers when meeting the leisure needs of twenty-first century boaters? One obvious answer is that canals do not exist simply for the pleasure of the boating fraternity. People on boats represent a minority among canal users. It is true that boats are necessary to bring the waterways to life, but on a recent trip on the Leeds & Liverpool I passed one other boat on the move, several anglers and even more people walking the towpath. Do the other users care about the historic landscape? It is, I believe, true that those who use the canal for pleasure genuinely appreciate this aspect, even if they do not necessarily formulate their ideas in words. I have no evidence to back this view, but one thing is clear: if the historic elements are removed, they cannot be replaced. No replica can ever achieve the special patina of time.

Another approach to restoration is to put the restoration of navigation as an absolute priority and to use whatever means are cheapest and most efficient to meet that end. An extension of this approach is the idea that where new buildings are required there is no point in simply imitating old styles. There is a great deal to be said for a genuinely modern approach, using modern materials in a contemporary manner. One of the most enthusiastic advocates of this approach was David Hutchings, one of the first to take over a successful restoration scheme, working on both the Avon Navigation and the southern Stratford Canal, thus opening up the Avon Ring. This story shows how many organisations were involved in so many different ways in getting waterways reopened.

The Lower Avon between Evesham and Tewkesbury had long been unnavigable, but was still in private ownership. The owners had no wish to restore it and no money to do so even if they had wanted to. In a remarkably bold venture, the

New developments at Paddington are well under way. The area has already seen the sweeping curve of the motorway dominate the canal, and now new buildings seem likely to make even greater changes.

Midlands IWA bought it for £1,500 and work began. It was soon realised that if the Avon could be restored all the way to Stratford, then the Ring became a real possibility, and would have a huge appeal for the new generation of holiday boaters. The trouble was that the Southern Stratford was in a deplorable condition and in 1959 Warwickshire County Council applied for permission to abandon it. This would have not only removed any responsibility for maintenance, but would have given them carte blanche to fill in locks, lower bridges or use the land in any way they saw fit. The law allowed them to do so, provided no boat had used the canal in the previous three years. They seemed to be on secure ground, since it was obvious that no narrow boat could have got through. They had not allowed, however, for one intrepid canoeist who had made the journey in 1957 and had kept all his toll receipts. Closure was illegal, and at this point the National Trust stepped in, leased it and authorised the start of restoration.

David Hutchings was one of those men who, once started on a project, charged straight ahead until the work is done. A work force was recruited, if that is the right word, since it included men from the army and the RAF as well as prisoners from Winson Green. The Royal Engineers rebuilt Chadbury Lock as a practical training exercise, for example. New locks were, in general, built as cheaply as possible on the very sound grounds that there was not enough money available to do anything else. This could lead to some difficulties for later users. The approach to Robert Aickman Lock, for example, is particularly difficult as it is set almost at right angles to the river channel. Given Aickman's reputation as an awkward person to deal with, it is rather appropriate. Having a mixture of old and new is not a recent development on the Avon. At Eckington, for example, the river is crossed by a medieval bridge, built of sandstone with low, semicircular arches. These spring at different heights from their piers, the central navigation arch being the highest, while the side arches emerge at water level. The nearby railway bridge is a typical design of iron girders on stone piers. A more recent contrast can be seen at Evesham. The lock arrangement is entirely conventional, with lock and weir side by side. As part of the restoration programme a new lock cottage was built. Land was scarce, so it was built as an A-frame building rising directly above the weir. It is a most ingenious and satisfactory solution.

The success of the Stratford & Avon projects was a huge boost to the whole restoration movement. Not everyone was able to draw on the kind of human resources employed by David Hutchings. The early years on the Kennet & Avon, for example, saw small work parties meeting at weekends, gradually clearing away the jungle that had grown up on some sections and beginning to tackle the problems of renewal. Those involved in those days enjoyed the experience, but it has to be said that progress was not very rapid. It often seemed, and may well have been true, that the process of decay was acting more rapidly than the work of restoration. One answer was to get a large number of people together at one time to make a real impact. An enthusiast, Graham Palmer, who in 1966 had started a magazine *Navvies Notebook*, organised 'Operation Ashton'. On one weekend in 1968, six hundred volunteers descended on the Ashton Canal in Manchester, removed an amazing amount of rubbish from the canal, which was taken away and burnt. By the end of the weekend, some 2000 tons had been cleared. It was a huge success, and as a direct result a new organisation was formed, the Waterways Recovery Group. Sadly, Graham died young, but he too, like Robert Aickman, is remembered in a lock name, this time on the Montgomery. Britain's economic downturn in the 1970s and mass unemployment was clearly bad news for the country, but paradoxically it was good news for the restoration movement. A new work force became available through job creation schemes organised by the Manpower Services Commission. As more canals were reopened, the advantages to local areas became ever more apparent. Where once estate agents had tried to disguise the fact that there was a canal anywhere near a property, their advertisements now loudly proclaimed the fact as a positive selling point. Local authorities started to recognise canals as valuable amenities, and new sources of funds gradually became available. One of the biggest providers of funds of recent years has been the European Union. Then another new source of capital appeared on the British scene. Where once canal societies sold raffle tickets to members and friends to raise funds, now money comes in from the National Lottery. The result has been a move in emphasis away from the amateur navvy and towards the professional contractor. The result has been more than just a speeding up of work, it has meant that no problem now seems insurmountable. Restorers, it seemed, could now go round, through, under or over any obstacle. It has marked what can reasonably be called a new age of canal engineering.

Throughout canal history, special arrangements have had to be made to meet changing circumstances. This is often the case during restoration, where canals have been blocked by everything from motorways across their course to whole new buildings constructed on in-filled sections. This was a problem which also faced modernisers such as Telford, and if one goes back to the improved new line of the Birmingham Canal, one can see how change has been almost continuous as the demands of the city and the needs of the boating community clashed.

When Telford was invited to come and look at the Birmingham Canal in the 1820s with a view to suggesting improvements, he was not impressed:

> Upon inspection I found adjacent to this great and flourishing town a canal little better than a crooked ditch with scarcely the appearance of a haling-path, the horses frequently sliding and staggering in the water, the haling-lines sweeping the gravel into the canal and the entanglement at the meeting of the boats incessant; while at the locks at each end of the short summit crowds of boatmen were always quarrelling, or offering premiums for a preference of passage, and the mine owners, injured by the delay, were loud in their just complaints.

His solution was the famous straight-line canal slicing through the wanderings of the old Brindley line, often in cuttings which at their deepest were as much as 70ft below the surrounding land. Certain new structures were necessary to cope with the changes. The extended system required a new reservoir at Rotton Park, but there was still a requirement to continue supplies to the old summit level. Water had

A restoration problem solved. The bridge at the tail of Lock E24 on the Huddersfield Canal was widened, leaving no room for gates to swing, so a guillotine gate had to be installed.

been pumped in by a steam engine, but Telford's new cutting was at a far lower level than the feeder, in a deep cutting. So an aqueduct had to be built to carry the navigable feeder across the new main line. The Engine Arm aqueduct is an unusual example of canal architecture which has turned its back on the ideals of the Georgians, and looks forward instead to the Gothic of the Victorians. The basic structure is simple enough, a cast iron trough carried on a ribbed iron arch, springing from stone abutments. But between the top of the arch and the trough itself is an iron arcade supporting the two towpaths, one to either side of the trough. This uses the fashionable Gothic motifs, of pointed arches with quatrefoil piercings in the spandrels. It is something of a curiosity, especially as the main road crossing of the canal nearby is altogether grander but lacks the decorative detail. Galton Bridge was completed in 1829 and named after Samuel Galton, a local dignitary, intellectual and a member of the Canal committee. The central cast-iron span of 150ft carries a roadway over the deep cutting. Telford did not even trouble himself to produce a new design, but simply used one from an earlier, successful bridge over the Severn at Holt. Perhaps he realised that the bridge was so majestic that it needed no further embellishment. It is rightly regarded as one of Telford's most successful and dramatic bridges, but it came with a built-in obsolescence factor: it carried a main road in an increasingly busy city. A bridge that was adequate for the first part of the nineteenth century was unable to cope with the second half of the twentieth. It was decided to replace it, but fortunately there was no question of knocking down Galton Bridge. Instead a new road was constructed at a lower level on an embankment. A huge concrete tube was set in the middle of this bank to carry the canal. It was a satisfactory solution in that the Telford Bridge has survived and the canal is still open, but it has reduced the majesty of the bridge, particularly when viewed from the canal.

Perhaps the best place to see how different generations have coped with changes in the transport system is in the area around Spon Lane. Telford had mostly met the old Birmingham Canal on the level, but not here. The new line was in a cutting, and the old route lay higher up the hillside. A junction was made between the old and the new through three locks, but the old line still continued blithely on its wayward course via the two-arched Stewart aqueduct, which became a canal flyover. On other canals, this would be an important feature, but here it scarcely registers, overwhelmed by later additions. Early in the twentieth century, new demands on the roads called for a new bridge to be constructed. The builders turned to a modern material, ferro-concrete. The design is unusual. The canal itself is crossed by a single arch, but half-arches carry the structure up to meet the slope of the cutting to either side. Vertical pillars carry the road deck, so that the bridge has a curious striped appearance. But even this is not the end of the changes on this one site. The M5 is the most recent arrival on the scene. The six-lane road is carried on five concrete piers standing in the middle of the canal. The bases are cylindrical and three massive struts rise up from each to support the overhead deck, dwarfing everything else in sight. What appears to be a new canal has also been constructed nearby, but is in fact a concrete drain carrying away water from the motorway.

Another Huddersfield Canal problem occurred at Slaithwaite, where the old had been filled in and a whole new canal had to be constructed, using modern technology but traditional cladding.

It is only to be expected that the demands of the modern age should necessitate changes in the two-centuries-old system. Within recent years, however, attitudes have changed. When the restoration movement first got under way it seemed like a permanent battle to preserve the best of the old from demolition. To the authorities, it seemed that canals were unfortunate anachronisms that should not be allowed to interfere with the plans for a bold new urban scene. It is easy to see how they were ignored. One of the most famous spots on the Birmingham canal scene was Gas Street Basin. You could walk the streets of Birmingham and never even guess at its existence. The only hint was a bright red wooden door set high in an old brick wall. The red was the give away. It was there to show firemen that they could open it and find water on the far side. In the same wall there was a half-concealed entrance to the basin itself, an enclosed, secret place with canopied warehouses closing in the views. I rhapsodised about Gas Street back in the 1970s, writing: 'Every city needs its Gas Streets: odd places, different places, not places done up for tourists, but there giving delight to the curious who take the trouble to look for them.' The words had scarcely been written before I received a phone call asking for my support in a campaign to preserve Gas Street, which had suddenly come under threat. I agreed, but the next morning the phone rang again: we were too late, the bulldozers had already moved in. For many years, Gas Street was open to the winds, until development on the site finally got under way. The view of the draughty car park was closed off by a new pub, which allegedly reflects the forms of the old buildings that once stood here. It does not. It seemed to me then, and still seems today to represent commercial development which pays lip service to its surroundings, but ultimately fails either to represent a building in sympathy with the best of the old, or to be bold enough to offer something strikingly new. I have no problems with what has been done at the M5 crossing. It may be considered brutal by some, but it is honest and undeniably dramatic. The Gas Street development is puny.

It seemed for a while that Birmingham, having shown a brief period of interest in the canal system, had forgotten it again. Then quite suddenly it seemed, Birmingham decided to reinvent itself as a modern city, where people could actually live as well as work. The centre which in daytime was the space squashed in between the ring road and its junctions and at night was all but deserted, suddenly came alive. There were major new and stylish developments: a magnificent concert hall, the International Convention Centre and the National Indoor Arena, and all centred on or near the canals. The area was revitalised and suddenly the canals were seen as amenities to be appreciated. Canalside cafes and restaurants joined the offices and shops, and opened out their faces to the water. New bridges linked the developments together. In 1950 Eric de Maré published his splendid illustrated book *The Canals of England*. In it he showed a photograph of 'sorry and unkempt' Paddington basin, and

Old meets new at Stalybridge: the squared off lines of the new bridge are harsh and further emphasised by the stone outlining. The horse was not enthusiastic.

contrasted it with a bright and cheerful barge café at a Gothenburg canal development. A sketch then showed, in a rather Festival of Britain sort of way, how an urban canal might appear. Birmingham might not resemble the 1950s sketch, but it does have the same atmosphere. The special quality of having water as part of a scheme has been recognised. Once again, the success is due to boldness of concept. The new has quality and is set off by the old. It is in fact remarkable just how well the old Horseley Iron Works bridges fit into this aggressively modern scene. But perhaps one should not be surprised: good honest design never goes out of date.

Other city centres have discovered the same secret: given prominence in development schemes, canals prove popular. It is far more pleasant and interesting to enjoy a drink while a boat goes past than it is to watch a truck sweep by. Even 'sorry and unkempt' Paddington basin is getting a new look, which at the time of writing is still under construction, so that it is too early to say what the end product will look like. Manchester, however, is very much more complete, and Castlefield basin presents a fascinating glimpse as to how an area can develop over the centuries. It all began as the terminus of the Bridgewater Canal, and by the end of the eighteenth century, there were three warehouses on the site. The last of these to survive was the Henshall Gilbert & Co.'s warehouse, usually known as the Grocers' warehouse, but even that was largely demolished in 1963. It was surveyed before demolition. It used wooden pillars and beams, and was built with two shipping holes, running under the building where boats could be loaded and unloaded by a crane, powered by an underground waterwheel. The end wall has recently been restored, with the two arches of the shipping hole clearly on view. The first big change came to the basin with the arrival of the Rochdale Canal, which joined the Bridgewater at the basin. This brought a big increase in trade, so that by the middle of the nineteenth century, there were half a dozen warehouses on the expanded basin, together with new wharves. Each was given a name indicating the commodities that were handled – potato, coal, slate and timber wharves. Two important warehouses of the 1820s have been recently restored. Merchants Warehouse of 1827, damaged by fire in recent times, is typical of its period. It stands five stories high, brick built with timber beams on cast iron pillars. Externally it has a regular pattern of windows, many of which are round headed, and loading slots on both the canal side and on Castle Street. Like the earlier warehouse it too has two shipping holes. Across the water, the Middle Warehouse is very similar in design. Now converted into apartments, it has lost little of its character, though the end gables have been glazed and dormers added along the roof to create the currently fashionable loft space. Change did not end when canal construction stopped. In the nineteenth century the railways arrived, and lines swept over the canal on some very impressive viaducts, four in all. The most striking was built in 1880 to reach the new Central Station. The construction was very straightforward in iron, but stone castellations were added to make the effect rather less stark. Under the viaduct a little cast-iron arched canal bridge looks quite dainty. This is one of the places where one can see the ideas of different generations of bridge builders, using a whole range of different materials. The latest addition is a modern pedestrian bridge, with the walkway slung from delicate arches. A rather more modest lifting bridge, built to a traditional design, spans the canal in front of the remains of the Grocer's Warehouse. The result of all this activity is an amalgam, where the buildings and structures of canal and railway engineers still survive in very recognisable form, but the use has changed dramatically. Pleasure boats use the canal, a modern light railway system now runs where once steam expresses thundered, and buildings have been converted to housing and offices. Castlefield, which was really rather run down has been regenerated, and the basin forms the centrepiece for an area crammed with bars and restaurants.

The success of developments such as Castlefield has certainly done the whole restoration movement a favour, by showing that canals can be enjoyed by all sections of the community. Nevertheless, they were built for traffic and the main aim of restoration is still to open up canals to boats. A new generation of restorers has faced challenges which would have defeated the early volunteers. Castlefield was finally reunited with the canal system of the east when the Rochdale Canal was declared officially open throughout in July 2002. I walked the whole length of the Rochdale in 1987, and two problems struck me as being not so much difficult as insoluble. At Failsworth, the Co-op had acquired land, filled in the canal and built a supermarket right on top of it; the M62 was also entirely blocking the waterway. The answer to the first problem is easy, if you have enough cash. The supermarket was bought, demolished and a new section of canal dug. I found the answer to the second, but did not recognise it. To get myself across the motorway, I had taken a diversion through an underpass which served a nearby farm. The restorers have rerouted the canal through that underpass and made new arrangements for the farmer.

Equally troublesome obstructions faced the restorers of the Huddersfield Narrow Canal, and demanded equally drastic action. There were few problems in the rural areas where locks had been cascaded and capped. They simply needed to be uncapped and put back into working order. But on the more urban section to the east between Slaithwaite and Huddersfield, there were a number of major problems. At the Huddersfield end two factories had been built across the line. No one suggested purchase and development, but an engineering solution was found instead. Lock 2E was removed altogether, allowing boats from Huddersfield to pass straight through to a new, deep channel. Excavations from Bates factory created a channel underneath the buildings, flanked by concrete piles. This was then roofed over to create a tunnel and a new lock 2E created at the far end. A similar solution was found for the next factory covering the canal, Sellars & Co. Steel piles were driven, the canal channel excavated and a concrete invert constructed. The whole was capped with concrete slabs. Once again, a lock had to be rebuilt, the new 3E being inside the factory. Because of the buildings up above, this new, short tunnel is far from straight.

Slaithwaite had buried the canal, and a whole new section was built right in the middle of the town. Here the problem was not factories on the canal, but an important road bridge at Platt Lane that had been lowered. Once again, the solution was to move a lock to provide enough headroom to clear the bridge. The bridge in the centre of the town also needed replacing. The engineering solution for today was to build a box culvert, using sheet piling and concrete. The canal in the town had long been covered in, so once again the answer was to use modern technology. The result was harsh, practical and unlovely. Then came the cosmetics, the addition of stone cladding. The end result is a canal that fits its surroundings. Slaithwaite is a typical small mill town, and the canal has been given an appropriate treatment with the cobbled surrounds adding to the effect. In a sense, it is dishonest, but few would want to take the scene back a step to re-expose the raw concrete. In a few years, one suspects that the work of restorers will have been forgotten. The stone will have mellowed, the cobbles will have worn, and people will cheerily talk of an 'unspoiled' early industrial townscape.

The work done on the most recent schemes has been more than mere restoration. In places, the engineers have created sections of wholly new canal. The task has been to marry the new with the old. What has been done on the Huddersfield and Rochdale projects has succeeded. Restoration and the creation of new solutions to old problems are the aspects of the canal world that get the publicity. But that is only a part of the story. All the new work is pointless unless the old is cared for as well.

7. Leisure and Conservation

The idea of conservation is comparatively modern and arose more or less at the same time as the use of canals for leisure. When canals were considered simply as transport routes, changes were made purely in the name of efficiency. The first generation of canal engineers had, in general, done their work so well that the original infrastructure has survived. Bridges, for example, might need patching, but seldom replacing. When improvements were needed, however, the canal companies used the materials and methods of their own age, with no regard for history.

When the Grand Union Canal Co. embarked on its massive modernisation programme in the 1930s, it celebrated the fact by issuing a handsome book, *Arteries of Commerce*. It still makes fascinating reading, not least for the detailed picture it provides of just who was carrying what by canal. The company's aim was straight-forward promotion. Early in the book, there are two photographs, before and after improvement. In the first, the canal looks almost like a natural river, the edges softened by years of growth, hedgerows lolling over the towpath. It all looks rather idyllic, and would certainly gladden the heart of any nature conservationist. That is not the company message, and one can see just why they found it so unsatisfactory. To them it speaks of neglect, of an old-fashioned system, unsuited to modern trade. The second shows the canal contained within new sheet piling topped by concrete, the hedges trimmed and pushed back behind new fences. This is the image of an up-to-date system, intended to encourage commercial traffic to use the waterway. Advertisers in the book were keen to reinforce the message. The British Steel Piling Co. Ltd praised their product as 'the most effective and economical method of constructing or reconstructing canal wharves'. L.J. Speight proudly displayed their work for the Grand Union, which included the construction of fifty-one new locks in concrete and three reinforced concrete bridges. To illustrate their success they used a photograph of one of their new masterpieces, Ugly Bridge. Irony was clearly not their strong point. Perhaps the most interesting advert is that for Davies Brothers of Wolverhampton, offering to build modern canal warehouses. The illustration shows a warehouse under construction on the River Brent at Brentford. It is 104ft long, 72ft wide and has a cantilever projecting 30ft over the canal so that boats can be loaded and unloaded under cover. The design is not new, but what is new is the material. This uses the modern building technique of constructing the entire framework in steel and then adding an outer cladding. With its built-in electric crane, the warehouse met the needs of the commerce of its day. It is an entirely sensible method of construction and, if it had been available at the time, everyone from Brindley to Telford would have designed their warehouses in exactly the same way: and if we still needed big warehouses along the canals, this is how we would

Willowtree Marina on the Grand Union has provided facilities available to the general public as well as the boat owners. The style is 'traditional' in having a pitched roof and gables, but has no relationship to canal style.

Lemonroyd Marina on the Aire & Calder was constructed in conjunction with a new lock. It is strictly functional – a boat park – but trees have been planted to soften it.

A new development at Market Drayton has supplied an opportunity for moorings out of the main line of the canal.

build them today as well. But we do not, which is why new demands have been placed on the system and the issue of conservation has arisen.

The Grand Union boasted the 'the old days of leisurely movement are gone for ever'. By travelling night and day, the new generation of motor boats could be expected to travel from London to Birmingham in fifty hours: 'Once the journey is begun, the arrival time can be accurately and confidently forecast'. But today, leisurely movement is exactly what draws us to the canals. We do not travel night and day, nor do we want to keep to any rigid timetable. The working boats have all but vanished from the Grand Union; the leisure trade has taken over. Shown the two pictures so proudly displayed by the company, we should probably opt for the 'before' not the 'after'. The need for efficiency and speed no longer exists, but a whole new set of requirements has appeared. In the working days, boats were either at wharves loading and unloading or on the move – and any days when neither activity was

117

going on meant poor trade and a lack of business. The private boat owner of today may take an occasional jaunt at weekends and perhaps one longer holiday a year, but the boat is likely to spend more time tied up than moving. Hire boats are often laid up for months on end. If the canals were not to be turned into linear parking lots, these boats had to be found homes of their own. The answer was the marina. Some of these have been created out of disused arms and basins, others have been specially excavated. Where an old basin has been used, it has often proved possible to adapt warehouses, stables and the like to meet the needs of modern offices. Elsewhere, it is rare to find a great deal of imagination in providing good design, and because marinas are by their nature tucked away off the main routes it is generally thought not to matter too much. In any case, the main visual impression is of ranks of boats lined up like cars in a supermarket car park. But a great many of the services that are considered essential for the holiday boater are found directly on the main lines, and some of these are less than romantic, ranging from rubbish disposal to the pump-out for the boat loo. These probably seem less important in the grand scheme of things than do huge marinas, but visually they can have a large impact on the canal scene. We shall be looking at how they are dealt with a little later on.

An important fact of life for most canal users is that they usually have to work locks themselves. It is generally thought by those who decide such matters that holiday makers want life to be as easy and trouble free as possible. It was decided many years ago that the 'old-fashioned' system of winding up paddles using a windlass to work a rack-and-pinion system should be replaced. The answer was the hydraulic paddle gear. This immediately raises a conservation issue. It is my belief that one of the delights of canal travel derives from diversity, the fact that each canal has its own identity and signature. The enclosed paddles of the Grand Union for example, look very different from the open gear of the BCN a little further along the way. Gearing on the Leeds & Liverpool, with its lever-operated cloughs, is different from that of the other trans-Pennine routes. These are all very obvious differences, but other, more subtle differences can be found throughout the system. The new gear is uniform, and anything that reduces variety and individuality is to be deplored. I would go further. It is ugly. The gear squats on the balance beam, like a black wart. There is a particular appeal in the traditional lock arrangements of the narrow canal. One can sense the thinking behind it. The Oxford Canal probably has as many good examples as anywhere. The arrangement is entirely logical. The upper gate can only be used when the lock is full, so it can sit on a sill. Being comparatively short, a single gate can easily be moved by the balance beam. When filling the lock, water needs to arrive at the bottom to avoid flooding the boat inside, so ground paddles are used. At the opposite end, the gates rise the full height of the lock, so two are needed to make the job of moving them easier. There is no problem here with drowning out the boats inside, so water can be released through gate paddles. This creates a satisfying visual rhythm, a balance of the strong horizontals of the balance beams and their hand rails against the rather spiky, contrasting verticals of the paddle gear. Hydraulic gear destroys that balance. The notion that in some way the gear makes for lighter work is of course fallacious. The effort required per turn of the windlass

The covered paddle gear adopted by the Grand Union Canal in the twentieth century establishes a bold visual rhythm at Bascote locks (above).

It contrasts with the traditional paddle gear on the Trent & Mersey. The appeal comes partly from the satisfying, sculptural shape, partly from the fact that all the workings are on view and, not available in picture, form the splendid noise they make (left).

There are two approaches to new construction on canals: pastiche or modern. At Apsley the new bridge is a triumph. It is, like the old bridges, using materials in an appropriate way.

may be less than with a conventional gear, but each paddle requires more turns. In any case, problems with rack-and-pinion only arise when there is a lack of maintenance and repair. There is another disadvantage. With the rack-and-pinion, once you have raised a paddle it is simple to fix it in place to stop it falling. I have many times cursed a hydraulic gear which, once raised, began to sink again – and there is nothing one can do to stop it. I have to confess that this is a hobby horse I have ridden many times – to no noticeable effect – but there is a serious point to be made here. The small things on the canal are every bit as important as the big.

There are certain aspects of the canal world that are outside the control of canal authorities. The canal corridor is narrow, and what goes on outside can have a huge impact on the experience of travel. The industries that line the banks have often been there for a very long time, deliberately sited to take advantage of water transport. They have been discussed many times in this work. Today, we live in a world where new buildings are much more likely to be offices than factories, though the latter have not altogether disappeared. There are examples of what has happened on or near the canal in plenty, particularly along the Grand Union. Ovaltine once had their own fleet of boats, so the canal was important to them. That may no longer be so, but the company still occupies a canalside site, though now with a modern building. The main structure sits four square and solid, but is well proportioned and has taken account of its setting. The glass façade both provides light for those inside, and reflects back the passing boats on the canal as well. Elsewhere buildings have risen in height, so that even if they are not directly abutting the waterway, they form the focal points in the landscape. There is a striking example where the Great West Road crosses the canal and a shining blue glazed tower rears up. The developers were looking for a good roadside site, and the presence of the canal played no part in their thinking. It is certainly not a bad building, but its presence has altered the canal ambience. This is bound to happen in a changing world, but just because the new tends to follow the latest styles of architectural fashion, has little concern for local identities and is based on standard units, it is all the more reason that the old should retain its quirky individuality.

Thanks to the restoration movement and the growth of the leisure industry, canals are busier than they have been for many years. Canalside sites are now seen as attractive. Builders of everything from offices to houses are keen to take advantage. In urban areas, change is inevitable and recent developments, such as those mentioned in the last chapter, give cause for optimism. I must confess to enjoying canals in towns and cities, but the increased use of canals and the scale of new developments inevitably bring conflicts of interest. There was a time when the waterfront at Banbury on the Oxford Canal was lined with typical canalside mills and warehouses, not to mention one of the very last of the old traditional boatyards. A

A new development, the Oracle Centre by the Kennet & Avon in Reading. The buildings are unashamedly modern, but sadly there is no chance of boats pausing in this narrow, fast-flowing river section.

large part of the complex was then destroyed to make way for a bus station. Then came redevelopment at the Castle Quay shopping centre. The buildings are deliberately modelled on older designs, with imitation covered hoists and a brick skin on the steel skeleton. Of course, if the old had not been knocked down in the first place, they could have been converted and we would have had the real thing instead of a pastiche, but that is water under the bridge. And water under the bridge caused a problem. There, in the middle of it all, was a typical Oxford lift bridge, an extreme irritation to the would-be shoppers who had to wait while a boat made its way through. Now three new bridges join the shopping centre to a new arts centre across the canal. The lift bridge is still there, or was at the time of writing, but no longer has any real function and looks sadly insignificant beside its latest neighbours. Change is not new in this area. The Oxford Canal had already been shuffled sideways to the north of the town, to make way for the M40 extension. We must expect more major changes to the canal environment over the years. Canals do not exist in isolation: the rest of the world will get on with its business all around them.

There has been an assumption made throughout this book that the canal environment has something special to offer that should be preserved. But is it true? There are many boaters who seem oblivious to their surroundings and ask for nothing more than to have water under their hulls and as few obstacles to progress as possible. We have all met them. Is there a case to be made for simply giving up the struggle, ignoring the past and accepting a watery rat race interrupted by McDonald's at regular intervals? Obviously, I would say no to that, but the negative needs to be justified. In the course of writing three volumes on canals and their structures I have been more and more convinced that they represent a microcosm that is worth preserving. No-one should lightly consign two centuries of history to the rubbish dump. The canals speak of an age when the world began to change, transforming itself from one based on rural life and agriculture to one centred on towns and industry. It had a huge impact everywhere, and those changes began here, in Britain. This 'new world' demanded a new transport system and the canals provided it. So the canals are witnesses to one of the great turning points in human history: they are of international importance. This is a historic fact which is at last receiving recognition, when places such as Saltaire and Blaenavon have been made into World Heritage sites. That puts them up there with the Taj Mahal and the Pyramids. And it is worth remembering that Saltaire is where it is because of the Leeds & Liverpool Canal, and the Blaenavon iron works depended on a tramway to the Brecon & Abergavenny Canal to provide a link to the coast. So that is the historical argument. That is only a part of the story. The canals have a sense of individuality and character that is lacking from too many modern developments. We are fortunate that most were built at a period which coincided with one of the great ages of British architecture, and much of that sense of style rubbed off onto the canals. So they have many intrinsic advantages, in that those who designed them worked with materials and in styles that speak to us as happily today as they did when they were built. Finally, each canal has its own character, seen in the big scale of the engineering line and major structures, but also in the details. Travelling by canal is

The boat approaching Greenberfield locks on the Leeds & Liverpool is heading straight for the white flash marking the navigational centre of the arch.

not like travelling by road, nor even by river. It is a unique experience. Whether walking the towpath or travelling by boat, one is reduced to human speed, not that of the modern world. There is time to look around, time to enjoy those small things as much as the great. I am personally convinced that care about the detail is as important as any other factor in both restoration and conservation. There was a time when this view was considered unimportant, and it has taken many years to get it accepted as vital to the continuing success of the canals.

A number of different elements came together to create the impetus for conservation. The idea of using canals for pleasure as well as commerce is a comparatively new one. Looking through the excellent bibliography of British canals compiled by Mark Baldwin, one is struck by the fact that before the middle of the twentieth century, the vast majority of the literature was of a practical nature. It was concerned with engineering, improvements, new plans for commerce; there was some history, but very little on pleasure boating. The history tended to be concerned primarily with company history, with a passing nod at engineering. What there was on pleasure boating on inland waterways was largely concerned with rivers and popular boating areas such as The Broads. Natural waterways had come into prominence, because they had been deemed worthy of regard by the writers of the eighteenth century who conceived the notion of the picturesque. Canals might occasionally be useful in getting from one river to another, but that was about it. There are exceptions, such as E. Temple Thurston's *Flower of Gloster* published in 1911, which took a view of canals not so very different from that of our own age, but they are few. All this has changed in the last half century. Today, the pleasure boat all but monopolises the canal system, and that has led to an inevitable reassessment of what the canal system should be. If trade on the canal depends on convincing the customers that the canal holiday is an attractive notion, then the canals themselves have to appeal in all kinds of different ways. They have to seem attractive in themselves, and they must offer an experience that is not available on other holidays. Taking a motor cruiser on the Thames, say, or the Broads is not the same as taking a boat along a canal. I would suggest that one of the crucial differences is the way in which the canal seems to take us back in time, its historical context. Another new element also appeared in recent times, the appreciation of industrial buildings, not just as relics of the past but as structures with admirable qualities of their own. One of the earliest, and still one of the best, statements of the new aesthetic was J.M. Richards *The Functional Tradition* of 1958, with evocative illustrations by Eric de Maré. Richards wrote enthusiastically about the clarity of the buildings, 'unobscured by the irrelevances of ornament', and many canal structures were included among the illustrations. Today, we are perhaps less puritanical in our views on architecture, rather more tolerant of irrelevant ornament, but we do still recognise an early industrial style which has its own virtues. By now, it should not be necessary to repeat what I believe those virtues are. Alongside this new appreciation of architectural quality, a new discipline was also being developed. Industrial structures were studied for the story they could tell about the industrial past. The discipline was given the name 'Industrial Archaeology'. The combination of these elements: new

No amount of reconstruction and restoration can reproduce the patterns created over centuries of use.

Tow ropes have carved deep gouges into the stone of one bridge, and even the metal bridge guard on the other has been cut into a comb-like silhouette.

canal users who wanted a visually satisfying background to their travels; an appreciation of the aesthetic qualities of early industrial building; and an understanding that such structures were historically important, led inevitably to a conservation movement. It took a little while for the movement to gain a voice in the offices of those who controlled the future of the waterways. The canals had never actually employed an architect in their first two hundred years. True, there were men such as Thomas Telford, who had considered a career in architecture, and had even designed two churches, at Madeley and Bridgnorth, before turning to canals, and others, such as John Rennie who showed a complete mastery of the language of fashionable classicism in his greatest structures. These men brought their architectural ideas with them, but they were employed primarily as engineers.

In 1967, a young architect called Peter White, who had his own narrow boat and had been on a watery pilgrimage following in the wash of Rolt's *Cressy*, undertook a new scheme in the heart of Birmingham. It was called James Brindley Walk, and incorporated many ideas that he was to develop over the years, notably a sensitive awareness of the qualities of the old while not being afraid to take a bold approach to the new. It was this that led British Waterways to appoint him as their first Architect/Planner. Peter and I first travelled the canals together in the mid-seventies, and I still have battered copies of the old blue-backed British Waterways inland cruising booklets with his thumb-nail sketches and notes. We have had our disagreements, but in general our views of conservation are very similar. The difference is that he views things with the eye of the professional architect, picking up details which I would certainly have overlooked. Here is an example from his own writing, where he was looking at how canal companies were ingenious in finding ways to save money without compromising the quality of the finished work. 'How on the Oxford Canal a certain half-lapped nailing of slates enabled far fewer to be used as a roof covering, how 'rat-trap' bonding also *saved* bricks because they would be laid not on a bed face but on edge, how brick wall copings often had a 'frog' created in their undersides (actually formed by a hand scrape whilst the clay was still wet) in order to *save* clay and to facilitate laying.' He felt that it was, in a way, as important to preserve such details as it was to keep a great aqueduct from demolition. It was not a view universally shared in the early days. The engineers were happy continuing the old tradition of opting for the simplest engineering solution, regardless of any other factors. One result of that approach can still be seen on various bridges around the system. The simplest way to preserve old brick and stone structures from wear and tear is to cover them with some form of weatherproof render, and many were sprayed with a material that when it set had all the charm of coagulated porridge. One of Peter's first and certainly most valuable contributions to conservation was the establishment of the *Waterway Environment Handbook*. This is not a conventional book, but a series of loose leaves in a binder, which can be

Opposite: The appeal of a canal lies as much in the small things as in the grand gestures, as in this beautifully executed overspill weir on the Macclesfield Canal.

One of the good things to emerge in recent years has been a wider appreciation of urban canals, as indicated by this plaque – no words are needed to tell us that this is on the BCN.

removed, replaced and added to at any time. Nothing was considered too big or too small for consideration.

When British Waterways first took over the canal system, they did what so many bureaucrats love doing: they imposed conformity. Everything was to be painted in the garish house colours of blue and yellow, and that even included the boats which got a new livery to replace the traditional hand-painted names and roses and castles decoration. That colour scheme was one of the first things to go, and few mourned its passing. There were now new rules to follow, but rules that sought to work with the individual identities of the different canals. So now, for example, colour schemes were tailored to individual canals: the front doors on all Oxford Canal lock-cottage doors would be painted the same colour, but that would not be the same as the doors on the Staffs & Worcester. It was standardisation of a sort, but standardisation that worked with the character of the old: the startling was replaced with the subdued. The same attitude was carried over to every kind of detail.

Under the new scheme, bridges were to be left with brick or stonework exposed, not painted. There were exceptions. For example, there is a tradition on the Leeds & Liverpool to mark the centre of navigation with a white flash on the arch. This looks slightly odd and lopsided, because it does not coincide with the actual centre of the arch itself, but marks the mid-point between the towpath and the far abutment. Iron bridges and aqueducts were to have their structures highlighted by the use of crisp black and white. But the mark of any successful scheme is that it leaves room for exceptions. The Engine Arm aqueduct in Smethwick is a good example (p.96). Its motif of pointed arches suggests the Gothic revival of the nineteenth century, so a colour scheme was selected that echoes that of the Victorian church. Peter has always been prepared to look at the old with a clear eye, to maintain diversity. In one of those old guides we used on our travels, I came across a marginal sketch of Bridge 104 on the Shropshire Union at Bunbury. It shows a typical turnover bridge, but what caught his attention was a recessed arch in the abutment that was used for storing stop planks. This is just the sort of elegant solution to a common problem – how to keep stop planks handy and well preserved – that delights him. He brought the same attention to detail to the modern waterways. Mooring rings are essential at locks and wharves. The Handbook recommends setting new mooring rings so that they are level with the surrounding surface, enclosed in a simple square of granite setts. You can use them, without tripping over them. Although there are designs for simple, new bollards in cast iron or concrete, the emphasis is always on keeping the old for as long as possible. It is easy to see why. Bollards change with use. Mooring ropes cut strange, spiralling grooves into iron bollards and wear away at wood. I saw a wooden bollard at the Hanwell locks, which had become so worn with use that it now resembled an overgrown egg cup. The effect is pleasing and sculptural.

We looked earlier at how the Grand Union Canal Co. was proud of their efforts to tidy up the canal in the 1930s. The holidaymaker does not want hard edges on his rural canals and we are now all very conscious of the importance of wildlife habitats. These are issues that are just as important as hard engineering. Where earlier a basin might have been created by simple vertical piling in concrete or steel, the new proposals called for concrete slopes which can be planted with reeds and grasses to soften the surroundings. Throughout the canal system, there are countless miles of hedgerows. These often provide the main visual background to our travels, but we may not think about them very much. They were certainly important to the canal builders. They were needed both to define the limit of the company's land and to stop animals straying from the surrounding fields. The easy answer to hedge cutting, which we see on roadsides all over Britain, is to drive a tractor down the length of it with a rotating cutter, leaving behind a massacre of scarred branches. The traditional method is more time consuming, but preferable in every way – hedge laying. Laying consists of partially cutting the vertical stems of the hedgerow shrubs, generally hawthorn, and bending them over before securing them with vertical stakes. The laid hedge will grow dense and uniform and will last for years, and if properly tended, for decades. It may seem that managing hedges has little or nothing to do with canal architecture and engineering. However, Thomas Telford was always most meticulous in laying down rules for hedges and fences, even going so far as to specify the plants to be used. If Telford did not consider it beneath his dignity to consider such matters, nor should we.

The Handbook does not limit itself to the preservation of old structures. It also contains ideas on how new developments should be handled. The modern holiday-maker needs a wide range of facilities undreamed of in working days, such as designated spots for rubbish disposal, sources of drinking water, fuel for the boat and

Very little is needed to fit new work into old, as here where a new basin has been created at the Brecon Canal terminus.

pump-out facilities for the loo. The best that can be offered generally seems to be some provision for hiding things away, behind shrubs and fences. The Handbook suggests ways in which this can be achieved. But if facilities are really hidden from view, then a new problem occurs: how to find them. A simple system of symbols has been invented to replace a clutter of wordy, printed notices. These are areas where the waterways authority often exercises a close control. In bigger ventures, such as marinas, that control may be lax to the point of non-existence. It has to be said that few marinas can boast buildings of any great quality.

All conservation is a compromise to a greater or lesser extent. The waterways have to meet the needs of those who use them today and who will use them in the future. A system built two centuries ago, is unlikely to meet those needs. The balancing act requires that the best of the old is retained, while the services for the new users are supplied. In the past, everything needed by the canal users was there on view, now we want to hide a lot of things away. It is not just a question of putting a screen fence round dustbins, it is also a question of finding a way of dealing with spoil from dredging. How these things are dealt with makes a real difference to how we perceive the waterways.

We need to face the fact that the growing popularity of canals is going to create new pressures. Having fought the battle to retain the special visual delights of the canal system, planners now have to cope with the demand for canalside developments. This is not new. The industrialists who wanted to build their factories with canal access were responding to demands in much the same way as a house builder who sees that he can get a higher price by having a canal at the bottom of the garden. Conservationists cannot settle for a status quo; they cannot freeze the system at one point in time. Equally, developers cannot be given a free hand to build what they want, where they want. It is all a question of finding a balance. If developers go too far, they will destroy the very environment that they wish to exploit. If conservationists are too conservative they will be in danger of turning the whole system into a historical theme park. In the past I have tried to predict the ways in which the canals would develop. I have not been very successful. Nevertheless, there are plenty of indicators for what might happen over the next few years. It would be foolish to try and predict further.

8. Canals in the Twenty-first Century

The big surprise of the early years of the new century has been the arrival of brand new canals, the first for over a hundred years. At the end of the year 2000, two major plans were on the drawing board: one scheduled for an early start, the other a formal acceptance of a project first conceived in 1995. The first to get under way was the Ribble Link, the second was the even more ambitious Bedford & Milton Keynes Waterway.

At the end of 2000, the Ribble Link was agreed in principle, funding was in place, but details still needed to be sorted. This is perhaps not too surprising, since this was a plan that had first surfaced in the eighteenth century. The intention then had been to link the Leeds & Liverpool Canal with the Lancaster Canal, but then that plan was changed to one which involved a tramway link. The whole story is given in detail in Volume 1. Changes over the years resulted in the Lancaster Canal being reduced in length and isolated from the rest of the system, ending at a terminus to the north of Preston. Now the dreams of the pioneers, of a direct link by water between the two canals, were finally realised. It is a mark of the new way of thinking that these proposals had nothing to do with earlier preoccupations. In the eighteenth century, the talk was all of trade, now the impetus came from one of the buzz phrases of the day, urban regeneration. Preston Dock had been one of those areas which had an unrealised potential, and a key factor in making it attractive to developers was the presence of boats. The Link would, it was felt, ensure that there were boats aplenty.

The modern engineers did exactly what their predecessors would have done, they looked first for a likely line. A natural waterway already existed, running north from the Ribble towards the canal, the Savick Brook. The Douglas joins the river well to the west of the Brook, leaving almost three miles of the tidal Ribble to be negotiated in between. Given that pleasure boats now regularly use tidal rivers, including the Trent, which offers a far fiercer challenge than the Ribble, this was not seen as an obstacle. The Savick Brook, however, did not look like a very promising basis for a navigable waterway. In its unimproved state, as it still existed at the start of the new millennium, it left the Ribble as a typical tidal creek running between glistening banks of mud, proceeded north, then turned east to wriggle its tortuous way across the countryside to a point near, but well below, the level of the Lancaster Canal. Nevertheless, the decision was taken that this would form the basis for the Link, when the first survey was carried out in 1981.

This is in many ways a remarkable canal, and one can see why the eighteenth century engineers would not consider it viable. It is only three miles long, yet the difference in levels between the tidal river and the Lancaster Canal required the construction of nine locks. One of the last decisions to be taken was to be the dimensions, and it was eventually agreed that they should be able to take both full-size narrow boats and the wide boats of the Leeds & Liverpool, so locks were built 72ft long by 14ft 3in wide. Once this decision had been taken, and the final, inevitable legal wrangles resolved, work began in the Spring of 2001. Everything was to be done using the latest and most efficient engineering techniques. The brook needed to be dredged to navigation standards and the banks consolidated. At places this required no more than providing an edge of steel piling, but in other places a rather softer approach was used. Instead of the hard, regular edges of sheet piling, gabions were set into the banks, essentially wire baskets filled with stones. They look just as crude as sheet piling when first put in position, but in time they mellow and plants can establish themselves amongst the stones. The locks are equally basic. Mechanical diggers excavated the chambers and again, sheet piling was used to create the walls. Without such modern technology, the canal would never have been completed as quickly as it was, with the first flotilla of boats setting out to cruise between the Lancaster and Leeds & Liverpool Canals for the very first time in July 2002.

Looking at the canal today, one can see just how daunting a task its construction would once have seemed. The nine locks include a three-lock staircase, to raise the new navigation up to the level of the Lancaster Canal. Designing this link must have led to a good deal of discussion, because the natural direction of the natural waterway does not head conveniently towards its artificial neighbour. So a turning basin had to

To create the Ribble Link, the engineers have made use of a modest natural waterway, the Savick Brook.

be dug, where boats could manoeuvre through a right-angled bend to reach the foot of the locks. At the top of the staircase the actual junction supplied a familiar problem. A new bridge was needed to carry the towpath of the Lancaster Canal. It provides an interesting mixture of the new and old. The span itself is built of steel, but it springs from concrete abutments. To blend these in with the more traditional canal scene they were given a brick cladding. The main material is Accrington brick, a somewhat lurid brick which can be seen in the cotton mills of Preston. It is offset by the use of hard, blue engineering bricks at quoins. It is not particularly elegant in its outline, but it blends in well with the older Lancaster Canal.

For a very short waterway, the Ribble Link is certainly not without interest. A new tunnel had to be created under the Preston to Blackpool railway. At the southern end, the tidal section of the brook is connected to the Ribble through a single-gate sea lock. Boats wait here on the Navigation until the tide rises to meet them. Without this device, they would be stuck on the mud flats until they floated clear. Perhaps the oddest feature stands by the top lock, a sculpture by Thompson Dagnall, *Gauging the Ripple*. Carved in wood, it depicts a very large, naked man and I feel disinclined to speculate on what he uses for gauging. It is too early to say how successful this new waterway will be, and in any case there are different criteria for measuring success. Canal enthusiasts will be looking to see how many boats make the quite tricky passage on the tidal rivers. In particular, they will want to see a revival in the fortunes of the Lancaster Canal. It is a beautiful waterway and has undoubtedly suffered from being isolated from the rest of the system. Others will be looking to see what it does to property values and development plans in and around Preston Dock.

The next new waterway also has its origins in plans that were first drawn up two centuries ago. In 1811 John Rennie was employed by a group of Bedford businessmen to survey a route that would link the Grand Junction to the Ouse at Bedford. The advantages for Bedford itself were obvious, as their only link to the main canal system was a roundabout route via the Bedford Levels to the Nene. Nothing came of the scheme, and there was a rather half-hearted attempt to revive it in the 1890s. By then canal construction was not on anyone's list of priorities, particularly as a railway existed over the route. The idea of the link was revived again in the 1990s by an IWA member from Cambridge, Brian Young. A Trust was formed, but at first there seemed no chance of raising the funds. Then, in 2000 British Waterways gave the plan their official blessing. This major step forward and the formation of a new partnership which included local authorities, development agencies and local boating societies, occured just before Brian Young's sudden death. There was now enough money to move forward to a feasibility study.

The plan calls for locks to be built to the metric size of 30 metres by 4.34 metres; that slightly strange width figure simply translates as the same width as those on the Grand Union main line. The route is not very different from Rennie's original, but that is still occupied by the railway between Bedford and Bletchley, so that the new one stays mainly to the north of the tracks. In the first version of the plan, it was intended to leave the Grand Union near Fenny Stratford. There are problems from

A new housing development at Milton Keynes complete with private moorings.

the start, with a crossing of the River Ouzel and the A5(T), before the canal can set off across country. More difficulties lie up ahead, with the M1 cutting across the path and even more worryingly Brodborough Hill. On the far side the canal will run into Brodborough Lake, which is roughly 40 metres below the crest of the hill. After that things become a little more straightforward as the canal will head north over comparatively level ground to a junction with the Ouse near Kempston Church end, to the west of Bedford. Subsequent revisions have left the central section unchanged, but there are now three alternative starts at the Milton Keynes end and three at the Bedford end. There are also more worked-out ideas for Brodborough with locks and a tunnel being proposed. So, at the moment, the whole plan is up for consultation, and the most optimistic date for opening is 2010 – provided something between £80 and £100 million can be raised. If the scheme does go through, it will be the single most important development for many years, opening up a whole new area of inland

The brand-new staircase at the top of the Ribble Link, approached by a very sharp turn only made possible by the small basin at the foot of the locks.

waterways for exploration. Inevitably people are already talking about a Fenland Ring, and there is certainly a great attraction in the notion of turning off the Grand Union for an exploration of the fens and even popping in a visit to Cambridge. The Fenland waterways easily get overlooked, simply because of their remoteness from the rest of the system, but there is a great deal to enjoy, and it is an area full of historical interest. Many of the waterways have their origins in land–drainage schemes. Reach and Burwell Lodes seem the quietest of backwaters now, but they were once busy with craft. There is considerable evidence of former trade at Reach itself, where the lode divides round a promontory offering an extended wharf area that is still known by the old name for harbour, The Hythe. The lode might well have been first built by the Romans, and the port itself is certainly medieval. There was a trade in many commodities from reeds for thatching to locally fired bricks, and increasingly as land was reclaimed, agricultural produce that could be moved by water. Small industrial settlements developed at the ends of lodes, for example at Burwell where there is evidence of industrial activity stretching back through the centuries. A two-storey granary, with massive buttresses, is clearly an early wharf building, and the chemical works, built in 1864 to make manure was built right beside the lode to be served by barges and lighters. Swaffham Bulbeck has an area called Commercial End, which was developed into a Fen port in the early nighteenth century by Thomas Bowyer, and though many of the wharf buildings have gone, a few remain, converted to other uses.

Pumping and drainage dykes helped form this landscape, and one of the lodes runs past the last remaining patch of unimproved fenland, Wicken Fen, which still has a charming little wind pump. Drainage on a far larger scale can be seen at Stretham, where a steam engine was installed in 1831. It was supplied by the Butterley iron works, founded by Jessop and Outram, providing a neat historical link. It is an attractive thought that all this might be one day within range of boats on the Grand Union; and, of course, the Fen boaters will have an opportunity to travel in the opposite direction.

Whatever happens to this ambitious scheme, it seems certain that the tide of restoration is flowing as strongly as ever. Inevitably, however, all the comparatively straightforward restoration jobs have been done, and what remains tends to be a set of canals which have suffered serious damage over the years, and have even been filled in for much of their length. The Manchester, Bolton & Bury is just such a canal. Look at a modern map and it is not difficult to see why, for it runs through almost completely built-up areas, and it has had a remarkably varied history. It was begun in the mania years, in 1791, with a name which explained just where it would be going – except that it wasn't. At first, the company were unable to make the necessary connection with the River Irwell to enable it to reach Manchester. This was not quite as bad as it might appear, as the canal's main trade was in coal, bringing it from the many collieries in the area to the cotton mills. It was originally designed as a narrow canal, but then the Leeds & Liverpool indicated that a junction between the two waterways would be mutually beneficial. The Manchester, Bolton & Bury Co. were sufficiently convinced to rebuild the locks they had already completed to a width of 14ft 2ins. Then the Leeds & Liverpool Co. decided they didn't really want a junction after all. In 1808, they finally got the land they needed, and completed the line down to the Irwell.

The canal as built was only 15 miles long, heading north west to Nob End near Little Lever, where it divided: one branch heading to Bolton, the other to Bury. There were seventeen locks to Little Lever, raising the canal 187ft and six aqueducts along the way. Water for the summit was supplied from the Elton reservoir, built close to the Bury arm. A useful addition came to the route when Matthew Fletcher built what became Fletcher's Canal to link two collieries, Wet Earth and Botany Bay. The former has a special place in canal history, as the pit where James Brindley was employed in supplying water-powered drainage. It was his success here that brought his name to the attention of the Duke of Bridgewater. Fletcher's canal was eventually to be joined to the Manchester, Bolton & Bury Canal by a single lock. The canal prospered until, inevitably, the railway came along. The old transport route was rather unceremoniously bundled to one side by the newcomer, with locks having to be realigned and the canal being pushed underground in a pair of short tunnels. It was the start of a long period of decline, speeded up by a number of collapses and land slips. The canal passed into railway ownership, eventually finishing up as part of the London, Midland & Scottish group, and the new masters had no appetite for expensive repairs: a familiar story. By the middle of the twentieth century the canal was scarcely useable and it was officially closed. The

The new and the old: a concrete arch on the Ribble Link (above) is plain and stark compared with the first bridge encountered on the Lancaster Canal, constructed of rusticated stone (opposite).

way was now clear for developers to build over canal sites and in general do as they would with no thought for any canal's future. The final death blow seemed certain with the announcement of the construction of the Manchester–Salford relief road. However, in the brave new world of canal restoration, nothing can be considered impossible and in 2001 British Waterways announced that restoration was now a real possibility and set up a consortium with local authorities. The immediate result was an agreement that the road builders would supply a navigable culvert, useable but not quite grand enough to be called a tunnel, under the road. This involved removing masonry from the old, derelict locks and setting it aside for future use. The threat was removed.

Removing a threat is an obvious necessary starting point, but the remaining difficulties seem formidable. Current figures call for an expenditure of £32 million. Why should anyone wish to spend so much on a canal passing through a region currently best known for old, failed industries? The answer says a lot about the ways in which attitudes have changed. It is not so much the value of the canal itself, as the land around it that is encouraging the backers. The old waterway will be the spine for new developments of all kinds; it is all to do with, in the most popular word of the day, regeneration.

The task is daunting, simply because so much has disappeared: locks built over, tunnels swallowed up, aqueducts demolished and a very large part of the bed filled in. The once imposing Damside aqueduct over the Tonge, for example, at least went out with a bang, demolished by explosives in 1965. Now only the abutments remain. It is hard to recognise now that this was once a canal with some very impressive engineering features, including a pair of three-lock staircases at Prestolee near Little Lever. There are survivors, however, including the three-arched Clifton aqueduct across the Irwell. This is one of the most interesting sites on the canal, which also saw the meeting of two rival railways, the East Lancs and the Manchester & Bolton, and the lines stride across the valley close to the aqueduct on thirteen arches. Here too is the junction with Fletcher's Canal and the Wet Earth site has recently been developed as part of a heritage trail. A number of bridges survive en route, mostly of brick. The line actually starts with a rather alarmingly named bridge that takes the Irwell Navigation towpath over the canal entrance. Bloody Bridge is not a joke name – it comes from a particularly nasty Victorian murder at the site. A number of town wharves have survived, as too has a splendid industrial relic at Radcliffe, the Mount Sion steam crane, built in 1875 to unload coal at the wharf. At this stage it is impossible to say how the restored canal will look, but it is unlikely to bear very much resemblance to the original waterway. In the language of the new officialdom it will be 'a key regeneration corridor, linking a series of inner city rejuvenation programmes' and will be 'a magnet for investment'. This is, like it or not, probably the only way the huge funds could be found for such a scheme.

Opposite: If the Milton Keynes link goes ahead, boats from the Grand Union Canal will be in easy reach of such appealing sites as Houghton Mill on the Great Ouse.

The St Helens Canal is arguably the first modern canal in Britain, but much has been lost. The basin above the old locks at Widnes is now a marina, used by boats from the river.

The idea that canals are positive assets which encourage developers to promote schemes along their banks has certainly caught on. It has recently been extended to what some would call Britain's first true canal, originally known as the Sankey Brook Navigation. It attracted little attention when the Act was passed in 1755, simply because it was called 'An Act for making navigable the River or Brook called Sankey Brook'. River navigations were not new, so this was not news. What was overlooked was the fact that, unlike true river navigations, boats were never intended to use any part of the Sankey Brook itself. The whole navigation was an artificial cut, though it was fed by the natural stream. It does, however, stay very close to the line of the brook, all the way from St Helens to the Mersey at Sankey. Then the canal turns west along the Mersey, with access to the river through a lock at Fiddler's Ferry. In 1833, the canal was extended to its new main junction at Widnes. There were originally ten broad locks on the canal, though two more, set side by side, were added to provide access at Widnes. There were also three short branches. The top end of the canal was abandoned in the 1930s and the rest in 1963. Because the canal was used by sailing flats, swing bridges were generally built, and few have survived. There are plans in hand to replace a demolished railway swing bridge at Spike Island, at the Widnes end of the canal, by a new swing bridge, simply because it forms a useful crossing point. It will probably be based on the successful design used on the Kennet & Avon, such as that at Aldermaston.

A certain amount of work has already been put into clearing the canal environment in St Helens, and it has gained added importance with the opening of a new museum, The World of Glass. Glass making began on the site in 1773, and as at Stourbridge (Volume 2), the advantages of a canalside site for bringing in raw materials, sand and soda ash with coal for the furnaces, are obvious. The glass cone which dominates the site dates from 1887. It looks a little like a pottery bottle oven, but operates quite differently. Men worked right inside the cone, taking the molten glass from the central furnace to blow and shape it. This is an important reminder of the close connection between St Helens' most important industry and the canal.

In general, the canal at St Helens still has something of a forlorn air about it, but in 2002 the local authorities began a feasibility study for further restoration as, inevitably, part of a regeneration budget. At the opposite end of the canal, the old canal entrances were reopened to create a marina for boats on the river. Now there are plans for a second bridge across the Mersey at Widnes, which would provide an opportunity for widespread development of the area, with, once again, the canal providing a focus. This is good news, for the junction at Widnes is a place of considerable interest. The two entrance locks are constructed of massive stone blocks, separated by stone piers with rounded ends jutting out into the tidal river. The rounded ends were practical not decorative, as entry to the locks was always difficult, and it was a good skipper that made it in without a knock.

This is a canal of considerable historic interest, and one structure gives it a certain poignancy. In 1830, the world's first railway to be worked entirely by steam locomotives for both goods and passengers was opened between Liverpool and Manchester. As though to emphasise the superiority of the new technology it swept over the Sankey valley near Newton-le-Willows on a splendid nine-arch viaduct. The viaduct, built of brick with stone facing provided 60ft of clearance to allow the sailing barges to pass underneath. A print of 1831 shows a passenger train steaming cheerily across the viaduct, while beneath it a flat makes its gentle progress with a single sail, its peak extended by a sprit as in the familiar Thames barges. Another, even less flattering, picture of the contrast between old-fashioned navigation and new steam railway shows boatmen pointing at the train while leaning against very rickety looking lock gates, where the gate paddles appear to be raised by chain and windlass.

Because of its isolation, this is a canal that is unlikely to be hugely popular with boaters, but it is of great importance in marking the transition from the river navigation to the wholly artificial canal. In fact, compared with what has been done recently, restoration presents no very great problems. Yet other canals, which one would have thought had gone for good, are moving forward. The Wilts & Berks was formally abandoned by Act of Parliament in 1914, after a less than glittering career. It was begun under an Act of 1795 and completed in 1810. It was to connect the Kennet & Avon at Semington to the Thames at Abingdon. It wriggled its way across the landscape for 51 miles, its progress punctuated by forty-five locks and apart from a certain amount of trade with the Somerset coalfield was never particularly busy. Then came the GWR and even that trade vanished, and the canal slipped into decline and decay. It is still possible to follow its course using Ordnance Survey maps,

The attractive bridge beside the Thames is the last reminder of the Wilts & Berks Canal in Abingdon – but although built by the company, it actually crosses the River Ock.

where it puts in spasmodic appearances as dotted blue lines, but in places vanishes altogether. The most obvious gap occurs where it has been entirely built over in Swindon. Even the most optimistic restorers have had to recognise that the local authorities are not going to dig a channel through their shopping precincts. There is another disappearing act at Abingdon. Casual visitors might think that they have found the entrance from the Thames when they see a single-arched cast-iron bridge complete with the statement in the casting that it was erected by the Wilts & Berks Co. in 1824 and cast in Bristol. This is not the canal but the River Ock. Of the canal itself, all that remains to be seen is a notch in the river wall a little further downstream, though an old warehouse has survived a number of transformations over the years, including time as a Hygienic Laundry, and the old wharf houses remain. Beyond that, however, the line of the canal is no more than a strip of grass between houses and road. Even where it has not been as heavily built over as this, the canal frequently vanishes, usually culverted under roads. There is one curiosity en route. The A420, near Shrivenham divides to go under the double arches of a railway bridge: one of those arches once carried the canal.

Given such a wealth of obstacles one might think that of all canals this is the least likely candidate for restoration, yet work is under way. The Wilts & Berks Canal Amenity Group was formed in 1977, with the ultimate aim to open up a route from the Kennet & Avon to the Thames at Abingdon and also to link in with the Thames

A problem: the Wilts & Berks comes to a dead end at Wootton Bassett. This is only one example of the canal not being merely derelict but overbuilt as well.

& Severn near Cricklade. At the time of writing the Waterways Recovery Group were well on the way to rebuilding the lock at the western end of the summit at Wootton Bassett. Some sections are in water, but using volunteer labour inevitably makes for slow progress. And even if work goes on at a reasonable speed, that still leaves the interesting question of what to do about Swindon sitting inconveniently in the middle of the line. The long term solution is to go round in a brand new canal. The obstacles in the way of a complete reopening are formidable, and one can only admire the optimism and enthusiasm of the volunteers. There is no doubt that today the big restoration schemes depend on big consortia, which must include the major local authorities if funds are going to be available for large-scale engineering works. Like the Wilts & Berks, the Thames & Severn moved steadily forward but the first discussions took place half a century ago. It was the first canal restoration scheme which hit on the notion of asking for funds from the public by using television's Sunday appeal slot. I presented the programme and I recall we were delighted with the response, which I remember as being several thousands of pounds. Good work has been done, but it is only now with the formation of the Cotswold Canals Restoration Partnership that there is a realistic chance of completing the whole task. The cost is no longer measured in thousands: £82 million is the current estimate! The completion of the Wilts & Berks will certainly not cost less.

The canal world can never be static. The construction of London's North Circular Road called for a new concrete aqueduct to carry the Grand Union. Now the road has been widened and a new aqueduct has been built.

This is the reality of canal restoration in the twenty-first century: big money to pay for big engineering projects. We must, however, never lose sight of the fact that restoration is not the same as conservation. Those who pay the piper still call the tune, and when development money comes in it is provided as often as not by those who have very little interest in the historic fabric of the waterways. Often the old will be preserved, because it is seen as adding a 'picturesque' touch, or will be adapted to feed the growing market for restored buildings. Others will, however, see the restoration schemes as providing building opportunities and sadly in modern Britain there seems to be a paucity of architectural imagination shown in any but a handful of schemes. If the Wilts & Berks is reopened, will it still be the Wilts & Berks or will it be, in effect, an entirely new canal, designed to meet the demands of boaters looking for fresh waterways to cruise?

I am not going to stare into a crystal ball to say what will happen on the waterways in the new age. In these volumes I have tried to explain in words and Derek has shown in pictures what we consider to be valuable and important. We should be grateful that so much has survived, and we can acknowledge with at least some confidence that the qualities of the best of the old have at last been recognised. But what we can also see is just how easy it is to swamp the old and diminish its impact. Putting a purely personal view, I am much happier seeing a wholly modern building, that is honest and reflects its own times, than I am in seeing a wan pastiche. A supermarket with imitation loading bays is still a supermarket: the nod at old styles simply does not work. But I would not want to end on a pessimistic note. My travels revisiting Britain's canals have been a real pleasure, and I have found every bit as much to enjoy as I did when I took my first holiday trip about forty years ago. And in that time, the scene has been transformed. I look back on delights that I could never have enjoyed when I began my canal travels. Crossing Dundas aqueduct, still to my mind the purest example of how practical engineering can be enhanced by the application of a classical architectural language, is an example that comes to mind. The drama of descending the long flight of locks curving past old warehouses and mills to the splendours of the Marple aqueduct is another. There are the surprises of seeing boats once again using canals such as the Huddersfield and the Rochdale, which I certainly believed had gone for good. The canal world is still strong and robust; and if there is one thing that writing these books have taught me it is that you never stop learning about it, never uncover all its secrets.

Gazetteer

The following list gives the more interesting sites to be found on the canals covered in this book. The standard Ordnance Survey system of grid references is used with one small variation. The first number quoted gives the number of the Landranger (1:50,000) map on which the feature appears. This is followed by either a four or six figure number. The former gives a reference to features such as flights of locks and basins that spread over a large area; the latter gives a more exact location for specific features, such as bridges and warehouses.

Chapter 1

Grand Western Canal	Tiverton Canal basin & lime kilns	181/9612
	Westleigh tramway bridge	181/069169
	Waytown tunnel	181/0719
	Wellisford incline	181/102217
	Nynehead canal lift	181/144218
	River Tone aqueduct	181/147223
Bridgwater & Taunton Canal	Bridgwater docks	182/2937
	Tone aqueduct	193/271254
	Top lock	193/232253
Rolle Canal	Beam aqueduct	180/475210
Tavistock Canal	Canal basin	201/4874
	Morwellham incline	201/445698
Tamar Manure Canal	Weir Head basin	201/436711
Bude Canal	Canal basin	190/2006
	Marhamchurch incline	190/2103
	Tamar Lake	190/2910
Liskeard & Looe Canal	Moorswater lime kilns	201/2364

Chapter 2

Birmingham & Liverpool	Autherley Junction	127/902021
Junction Canal	Lower Avenue bridge	127/889075
	Watling Street aqueduct	127/873108
	Shelmore embankment	127/8021
	Norbury junction	127/793228
	Grub Street cutting	127/7824
	Shebdon bank	127/7426
	Woodseaves cutting	127/6930
	Tyrley locks	127/6832
	Audlem locks	127/6639
	Nantwich aqueduct	118/642527
	Bunbury locks	117/5759
	Ellesmere Port	117/4077
Macclesfield Canal	Red Bull aqueduct	118/830549
	Congleton changeover bridge	118/865621
	Dane aqueduct	118/906653
	Bosley locks	118/9065
	Marple junction	109/962884

Chapter 3

Regent's Canal
As Ordnance Survey maps are of very little help in Greater London, readers will find it easier to locate sites using an A–Z or similar street map.

Royal Military Canal	Iden lock	189/937244
	Scots Float	189/932227
Wey & Arun Canal	North Heath tidal lock	197/038214
	Drungewick aqueduct	187/0630
Pocklington Canal	Canal Head	106/800473
Carlisle Canal	Port Carlisle	85/2462

Chapter 4

Aire & Calder Navigation	Goole Docks	112/7422
	Ferrybridge Power Station	105/4825
	Leeds wharves	104/2933
Sheffield & South Yorkshire Navigation	Keadby junction	112/835113
	Swinton lock	111/465990
	Tinsley locks	111/3990
	Sheffield basin	111/8837
Weaver Navigation	Weston Point docks	108/4981
	Anderton lift	118/647753
Manchester Ship Canal	Barton swing aqueduct	109/768976
Oxford Canal	Newbold tunnel	140/4877
	Hillmorton yard	140/538747
Grand Union Canal	Foxton inclined plane	141/6989

Chapter 5

Forth & Clyde Canal	Bowling basin	64/4473
	Merryhill locks	64/5669
	Port Dundas	64/5966
	Dullatur embankment	64/7476
Union Canal	Falkirk wheel	65/8580
	Slateford aqueduct	66/221708
	Almond aqueduct	65/105706
	Avon aqueduct	65/967758
	Linlithgow Canal Museum	65/001769
	Falkirk tunnel	65/8878
Glasgow, Paisley & Ardrossan Canal	White Cart aqueduct	64/494634

Chapter 6

Lower Avon Navigation	Eckington bridge	150/922423
Birmingham Canal	Rotton Park reservoir	139/0487
	Engine Arm aqueduct	139/015889
	Galton bridge	139/015893
	Stewart aqueduct	139/002898
Huddersfield Narrow Canal	New cutting	110/0813

Chapter 7

No entries

Chapter 8

Ribble Link	Entrance lock	102/481289
Manchester, Bolton & Bury Canal	Irwell aqueduct	109/752063
Sankey Brook	Widnes locks	108/5184
	Sankey viaduct	108/578947
Wilts & Berks Canal	Abingdon bridge	164/497968

Index